Outdoor holidays for indoor people

Heinz and Geneste Kurth
OUTDOOR HOLIDAYS
for indoor people

The authors are especially grateful to Gordon Fielden,
whose generous help with the manuscript and readiness
to answer endless questions about his own experiences
of camping contributed greatly to this book.

Other titles in the series
By Heinz and Geneste Kurth
BARBECUE and the joy of cooking on an open fire

Text and illustrations © Heinz and
Geneste Kurth 1983
This paperback edition published and distributed in Great
Britain in 1983 by the Automobile Association, Fanum House,
Basingstoke, Hampshire RG21 2EA
Casebound edition published by B. T. Batsford Ltd.
Created and produced by Ventura Publishing Ltd.,
44 Uxbridge Street, London W8 7TG

ISBN 0 86145 173 2
AA Ref. 64842

Filmset by Keyspools Ltd.,
Golborne, Warrington
Colour origination by D.S. Colour
International Limited, London
Printed in Spain by Editorial
Fher SA, Bilbao

contents

Should you pack up and go?

The history of exploration is full of stories of intrepid heroes hacking their way through the African jungle, plodding up Himalayan mountainsides and wearily manhauling their sledges across the endless Antarctic wastes. We love to read about such stirring adventures when we are safely curled up in our armchairs. But we notice that many of the explorers lived in tents during their expeditions; that pythons sometimes slithered in under the canvas, that avalanches swept away their basecamps and that some of them were caught in blizzards and only discovered years later, frozen to death in their sleeping bags.

Unfortunately, such stories do not encourage us to abandon our armchairs and set off on an outdoor holiday ourselves. Yet the picture they present is a false one. Snowbound explorers may have suffered great hardships in the past but we know how to manage things better nowadays. Outdoor holidays based on camping, caravanning or touring the country in motorhomes have become a highly developed industry and choosing this type of holiday no longer means steeling oneself to face up to danger and starvation.

Roughing it in comfort
Far from being a starving explorer, the modern camper is more like the cosseted king in the picture opposite, his tent surrounded by helpers whose main purpose in life is to keep him as happy and comfortable out of doors as he would have been back home in his royal palace. There are now hundreds of specialist manufacturers turning out high quality equipment for the holidaymaker; thousands of first class campsites with excellent facilities; and dozens of camping clubs, hire firms and travel companies all offering their services. Almost the only difficulty that faces the pampered camping-customer is to decide exactly which type of holiday will suit him best and just how many home comforts he would care to take along with him.

Of course, there is still a romantic or a sporting side to camping too. Some people still prefer to sleep out under the stars, to bivouac on a rock shelf half way up Mount Everest or to take their early morning dip in an icy stream. But these things are a matter of personal choice and it is usual to begin more gently. If you are thinking of taking a camping holiday for the first time, you can be confident that with a certain amount of planning you will have as carefree and comfortable a time as you have ever experienced, and some of the ways of achieving this are outlined in the following pages.

Why choose an outdoor holiday?

To begin with, there has to be a motive for selecting an outdoor holiday. Why live in a tent, caravan or motorhome when there is the alternative of living in a high class hotel?

If you are like the majority of people, the answer to this question is initially a matter of cost. Hotels are expensive, especially for large families, and now that annual holidays tend to last for three or four weeks, not many families feel that they can afford to spend the whole of that time at an hotel. Accommodation for an outdoor holiday may cost less than a tenth of accommodation in an hotel, so that what is saved on overnight charges can be spent on sightseeing, entertainment or dining-out – or simply not spent at all.

You may also be the type of person who feels out of place in hotels. Often the atmosphere there seems to belong to the age of household servants rather than to

the age of self-service and do-it-yourself. Maybe you hate it when your children cannot be allowed to act naturally for fear of disturbing the other guests. Maybe you also hate having to dress for every meal. In that case you are likely to feel much more at ease on an out of door holiday. When living in a tent or caravan there is a greater sense of freedom and relaxation; children suffer from fewer restrictions; there is less fuss about clothes; breakfast can be taken in a swimsuit; there are no set mealtimes and so on.

An outdoor holiday can be a lot healthier too. City dwellers who normally spend their working day cooped up in a stuffy office can be refreshed and revitalised by a few weeks of open air life. It can be very beneficial to experience the element of back-to-nature that belongs to a camping holiday – the tendency to eat and sleep according to the body's natural rhythms, to go to bed soon after dark and rise when the sun warms up, to exercise unused muscles on small everyday tasks such as fetching drinking-water. It is even good to be in a place where the telephone cannot suddenly ring and create its own form of modern-day tension.

Above all, an outdoor holiday can be very flexible. If you have a tent or caravan of your own, it is seldom necessary to book a pitch in advance. There are sufficient organised campsites in most countries for you to be able to pick and choose and to move on to the next one if the first one turns out to be too full. You can penetrate into more rural areas where hotel accommodation scarcely exists; you can stay nearer to uncrowded beaches; you can move around from place to place; and you can even return home if the weather is not to your liking, without being obliged to pay the hotel bill for the rest of the week. More likely, you can suddenly decide to extend your holiday for an extra few days when you find that you are enjoying it and that the cost is not prohibitive!

Deciding which holiday to take

Once you have decided that you would like to try an outdoor holiday, you may be tempted to plunge in at the deep end. You may want to go back to nature, enjoy all the extremes of freedom, explore the wilds of Alaska or, at the very least, witness the first rays of the sunrise from the summit of the Matterhorn. These things can of course be done, but it is essential to gain some experience first, otherwise you might end up like Captain Scott!

The 'deep end' of outdoor holidaying is lightweight camping – when everything you need is carried either on your back or in cycle panniers and you learn how to perform ingenious feats with two sticks and a sheet of tinfoil. Lightweight camping provides the sort of holiday which is more like an expedition and the pleasure and sense of achievement that this gives are enormous. But it is something to be worked towards rather than started with and it should be tackled only by fit individuals who are seeking adventure rather than comfort.

It is in fact very common for young people suddenly to be bitten by the lightweight camping bug in their late teens, so one of the most helpful things that parents can do for their children is to take them on less strenuous forms of outdoor holiday at an early age. In this way they learn to stay warm and dry and well fed under the sort of improvised conditions that they have never had to deal with in a centrally-heated house. When they try backpacking later on they are then more able to cope with its rigours and special techniques.

Another kind of 'deep end' is the financial one. There are some very large and luxurious caravans on the market equipped with refrigerators, cookers, strip

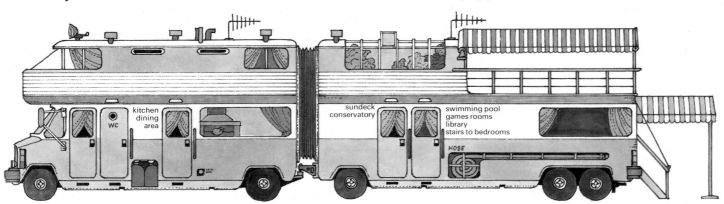

lighting, soft beds, toilets and almost more modern conveniences than are found in the average permanent home. But these cost several thousands of pounds and it is clearly not wise to invest in one before you have had some experience of towing and staying in a caravan and are sure of your requirements.

If you feel that soon you might want to buy a caravan, you should try to take an outdoor holiday in one that is owned by somebody else, in order to find out how much you like it. Or it might even be a good idea for you to try out a large tent or a trailer tent beforehand as these can be both cheaper and more spacious than a solid-walled caravan. There would be no sense in paying the extra money for a caravan if you found that, say, a cottage-style tent gave you everything you required.

Finally, there is that ultimate go-anywhere vehicle, the multi-purpose motorhome – usually a standard commercial van which has been 'converted' for cooking and sleeping in. Most of these vehicles represent some sort of compromise between what is an acceptable size of snail-house to trundle along the highway and what is a large enough space for comfortable living. If you feel that eventually you would like to own a motorhome of your own, spending a holiday in a tent is not going to simplify your choice, but you should try to visit a camping and caravanning exhibition or a dealer with a large stock. You could also try staying at a large campsite close to a trunk road. It might give you the opportunity to inspect a number of motorhomes while they are actually being used and to have a friendly talk with the people who are living in them.

On the other hand, it may be more helpful for you to hire a motorhome and see what it is actually like to live in; and you should try to judge how convenient it is to drive and maintain all the year round, not just in the summer.

Camping by car

Hiring a tent on site

For a first-time camping holiday it is not absolutely essential to own a tent of your own. The initial large outlay can be avoided – or postponed – by either borrowing or hiring one, or by taking a package holiday based on camping accommodation.

Borrowing a tent from friends has the drawback that however careful you are it is likely to suffer from a small amount of wear and tear while you are living in it. A zip may break, the seagulls may use it as a target or quite simply the sun is liable to make the canvas fade slightly. If your friends' tent is virtually brand new, it might be better to decline their kind offer to lend it to you for the sake of not losing their friendship afterwards! At most you could perhaps practise putting it up in the garden and sleep in it for a night or two, simply to get the feel of living under canvas.

For the actual holiday, probably the most trouble-free way to go camping is to purchase a package which provides accommodation in a ready-pitched tent containing all the beds and cooking equipment for a party of up to six people. Several tour operators offer this type of package and for car-owners in Britain there are bargain holidays on the Continent which include the ferry across the Channel in their price. A typical one would be at a carefully-selected campsite in the Châteaux country of the Loire, with a basic seven nights' stay in a large frame tent. The illustration opposite depicts the type of equipment which this deal provides – and incidentally serves as a guide to some of the main items that a family should take along on a camping trip when travelling independently.

Taking it all with you

As an alternative to staying in a ready-erected tent, it is possible to hire the tent and other equipment before setting off from home. This has the advantage that you are not tied to staying at a particular campsite and it also disciplines first-time campers into cutting down on the amount of baggage that they take with them.

Considering the huge packing problems that the beginner faces, he might wonder exactly where the advantage of the latter lies, but it is an odd fact that above a certain basic level the family's comfort and happiness on holiday do not increase in proportion to the weight of paraphernalia that has been dragged along.

Given a spare cubic metre of space, some business-men would even try to take along a dictating machine and a filing cabinet on the offchance that they might find time to send Miss Carstairs a few letters to type.

But they are much better off without such worries – just as their wives are better off when no one can expect them to conjure up a seven-course dinner on a two-burner stove.

The factor which clearly limits the amount of baggage that can be taken is the form of transport that the holidaymaker is going to use. For most campers this means that the limits are set by the size of the family car. If only two people are travelling, the problems are not so acute because virtually the whole of the back seat area can be filled with gear as well as the car's boot, but if all the seats are occupied then there is a real need to economise on weight as well as bulk. Some of the largest frame tents weigh over 60kg/132lb and occupy three lumpy valises, so clearly the owner of a mini should avoid hiring one of these, otherwise he might have to leave his passengers behind.

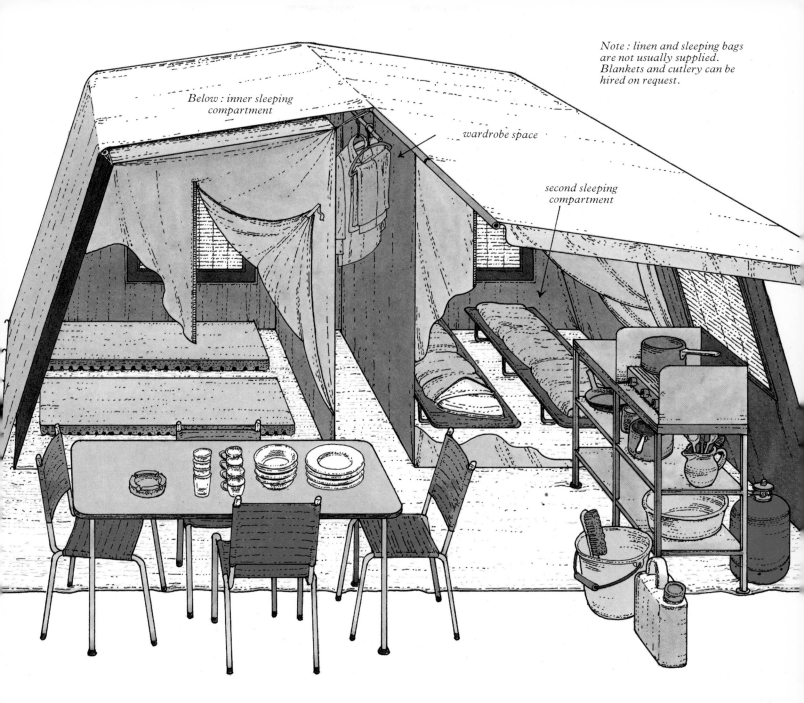

Note : linen and sleeping bags
are not usually supplied.
Blankets and cutlery can be
hired on request.

Below : inner sleeping
compartment

wardrobe space

second sleeping
compartment

13

1 table and chairs
2 bedding and beach towels
3 provisions and utensils
4 cooker unit
5 bucket and pans
6 clothing and personal items
7 groundsheet
8 tent poles
9 outer and inner tent

Full up inside

The first principle when planning what to take on holiday is to try and carry only as much equipment as can be packed into the boot, but if necessary a few safe items can be stowed in the passenger compartment. The tent's groundsheet, for instance, can be folded flat and placed on the floor under the front passenger's feet and the tent itself can be rolled up and wedged into the footwell between the rear passengers; or, with the sharp-pointed tent pegs removed, it can serve as quite a comfortable armrest provided that it is not liable to fly around when the driver brakes suddenly.

When the boot is being packed, some effort should be made to place heavy objects close to the car's axle so that they do not affect the ride or the steering balance. Items that are going to be needed first should also be packed last so that they can be reached easily.

Unfortunately, the sack containing the tentpoles is often quite a cumbersome object, over a metre (1.1 yd) long and about 30 cm (11 in) in diameter, so the tendency is to hide it away at the bottom of the boot. This causes some upheaval on arrival at the campsite because the frame is usually the first part of the tent that needs to be erected.

For carrying small expendable items such as packets of food, cardboard cartons obtained free from the local supermarket are perfectly adequate. They are lighter than proper suitcases or holdalls, and when they are empty they can be put to use as waste baskets and later thrown away. A single tall carton can also serve as a container for all the family's shoes, sandals and walking boots, which otherwise can never be found in pairs when they are stuffed into odd corners of the car.

More room on top

If boot-space is inadequate even after efforts have been made to economise, additional baggage can be carried on a roof rack. Items carried in this way, however, should be reasonably light and streamlined and they should be secured against wind and rain, and against falling off or being stolen. At motorway cruising speed the head-on force of the airstream is considerable, so objects that are large and square at the front will actually hold the car back and raise petrol consumption. If the expenditure is justified, special moulded cases are available for fitting onto a car roof; or there are strong bags made of waterproof fabric which also cut down wind resistance. More simply, the ground sheet of the tent can be wrapped around everything and tied securely, although there is a definite risk of tearing if the job is not done carefully.

Another one behind

Finally, for large families – or for people who cannot help being too big for their boots! – there is the possibility of towing a camping trailer. Since this adds to the length of the car it makes ferry-crossings more expensive and there are speed restrictions that have to be complied with in some countries. But small trailers are not difficult to tow and are invaluable for transporting more than one tent or, for instance, a couple of folding canoes. For storing at home they can be stood on end so that they do not take up too much garage space.

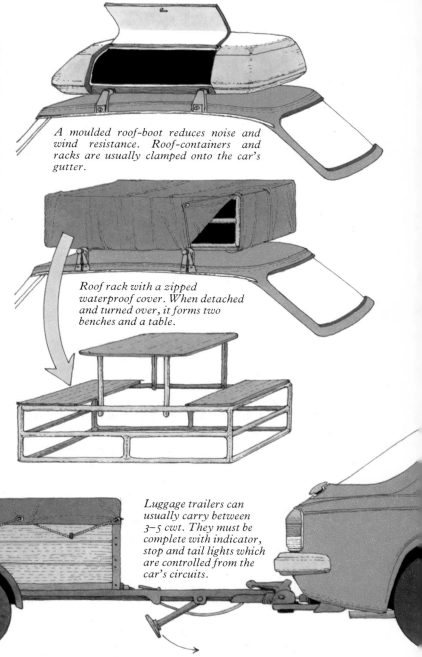

A moulded roof-boot reduces noise and wind resistance. Roof-containers and racks are usually clamped onto the car's gutter.

Roof rack with a zipped waterproof cover. When detached and turned over, it forms two benches and a table.

Luggage trailers can usually carry between 3–5 cwt. They must be complete with indicator, stop and tail lights which are controlled from the car's circuits.

Beds and mattresses

However little space there is in the car, there are a number of items that are essential for a comfortable camping holiday and unless these are being hired at the campsite – which is only rarely possible – they have to be obtained in advance and taken along with you. At the top of this list of essentials are beds and bedding.

So shall you lie

People who have never been camping before have visions of spending cold, sleepless nights on the bone-hard ground and indeed this is a hazard that must be avoided at all costs. Nothing is more likely to ruin the enjoyment of an outdoor holiday than lying awake in the dark feeling frozen and imagining that every

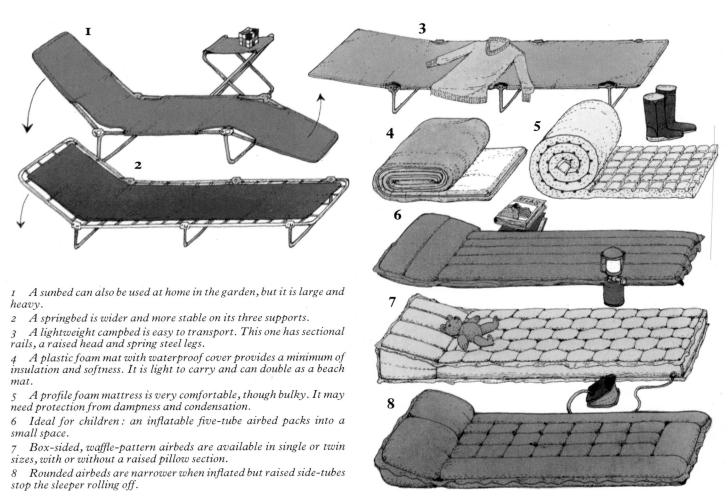

1   A sunbed can also be used at home in the garden, but it is large and heavy.

2   A springbed is wider and more stable on its three supports.

3   A lightweight campbed is easy to transport. This one has sectional rails, a raised head and spring steel legs.

4   A plastic foam mat with waterproof cover provides a minimum of insulation and softness. It is light to carry and can double as a beach mat.

5   A profile foam mattress is very comfortable, though bulky. It may need protection from dampness and condensation.

6   Ideal for children: an inflatable five-tube airbed packs into a small space.

7   Box-sided, waffle-pattern airbeds are available in single or twin sizes, with or without a raised pillow section.

8   Rounded airbeds are narrower when inflated but raised side-tubes stop the sleeper rolling off.

unfamiliar sound means that your tent is surrounded by abominable snowmen. Not only is this kind of martyrdom unnecessary, but snuggling down into a warm sleeping bag at night and waking up slowly in the morning with the sun turning your tent into a cosy cocoon must be one of the most luxurious experiences on earth, so it makes sense to take along comfortable bedding and give yourself a chance to enjoy it!

The main difference about sleeping in a tent from sleeping in a house is that the thin tent walls do not retain any of the sun's daytime heat, so bedding needs to be rather warmer than at home. The ground underneath the tent also becomes quite cold at night, so you will need to insulate yourself from it as much as possible. One way of doing this is to take along a type of bed that raises you off the ground (see illustrations). The alternative is to use a mattress that lies directly on the floor of the tent but which insulates the sleeper by placing a layer of air or air-filled foam between him and the cold ground (see illustrations).

Of the various types of mattress, box-sided airbeds are probably the most satisfactory of all. They are deep enough to provide good insulation and wide enough to allow the sleeper to move about on them, and if they are not over-inflated they provide the same combination of softness and support as an ordinary domestic bed. Because of their large surface area, they are also less likely to slide about on top of a smooth groundsheet even if the ground where the tent has been pitched happens to have a slight slope.

Dealing with inflation

Airbeds do, however, have to be pumped up, so an extra piece of equipment is needed: it is not wise to inflate them by mouth because moist breath may eventually cause them to go mouldy inside. Inflators come in various styles and sizes and a selection is shown below.

The type which runs off the car battery saves a great deal of effort, especially when a whole family is touring and several beds have to be blown up afresh each evening, but it is as well to have a non-electric pump as a back-up system. The leads connecting an electric inflator to the car battery may not always be long enough to reach into the tent from where the car is parked, and this makes things difficult when it is raining. Some inflators of this type are also rather noisy, which makes them unsociable to use late in the evening on a quiet campsite.

Finally, in case an airbed becomes damaged it is sensible to carry a small repair kit – some manufacturers supply one, and a spare stopper.

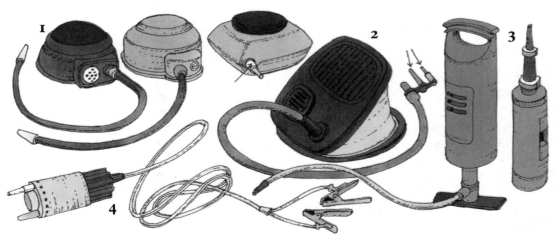

1 Domed rubber inflators are easily operated with the foot.

2 A larger bellows-type footpump delivers more air per stroke.

3 A handpump delivers air on both the up and down stroke.

4 12-volt inflator works off the car battery.

17

Quilt-type sleeping bags

As far as bedding is concerned, ordinary household sheets, pillowcases, blankets, quilts etc. are usually too sensitive to be used for camping. They are also rather bulky. Instead of separate items of bedding, it is more practical to have a one-piece sleeping bag that will not suffer as a result of being trampled on or crammed into the car boot. It also provides the right kind of warmth because the way to ensure a comfortable night's sleep is to have as much insulation underneath your body as on top of it. Neither an air mattress nor a thin campbed gives enough warmth by itself.

Hitting the right sack

The choice of sleeping bags available is very wide. Many of them are specially designed for lightweight camping (see page 56) and they can be rather expensive, but for car holidays the ordinary oblong quilt-type sleeping bags are perfectly adequate. For adults they come in two sizes, standard and king size, with approximate measurements of 183 × 84 cm (72 × 33 in) and 198 × 96 cm (78 × 38 in). There is also a junior size which is about 137 × 55 cm (54 × 21 in). In all cases the filling consists of a man-made fibre such as Terylene which is a good insulator even when compressed, and the weight of filling is traditionally quoted as '38 oz' (1 kg) or '44 oz' (1·25 kg). Unless a tog rating is also given, however, this weight is not a true guide to the bag's insulating properties: because of the extra surface area, a king size bag is no warmer than a standard size bag.

For most adults, king size is a better buy because the extra length allows the bag to be wrapped more closely around the shoulders. Other points to consider when buying a sleeping bag are the type of material used for the lining (cotton is more comfortable than nylon); whether there is a gusset covering the zip (which helps to prevent cold spots); and whether the bag is washable (with dry cleaning, special care has to be taken to ensure that no poisonous fumes remain trapped in the fibre filling).

To complete the sleeping equipment, one or two spare blankets are helpful at chillier times of the year and a large beach towel can double as a sheet for covering a slippery nylon mattress. Pillows are usually improvised out of items of clothing – it is quite handy to fill a small cushion cover with clean socks and underwear and use that as a headrest. Alternatively, inflatable pillows can be bought but experienced campers tend to prefer dual-purpose items: a hot water bottle, for instance, makes quite an acceptable pillow when it is inflated with air or after it has warmed up a bed.

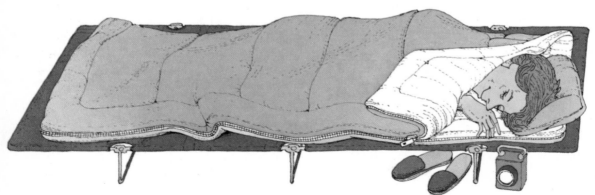

Quilt-type sleeping bags have a continuous zip along the foot and side which enables them to be opened out as a quilt, or linked together to form a double bag.

The package holiday mentioned earlier provided accommodation in a frame tent, and it is this type of tent which most families choose to own if they regularly go camping by car. With reasonable care, a good quality tent will last for many seasons, so it is certainly worth investing in one as soon as you have made up your mind that camping holidays suit you. For those who are uncertain at first whether to hire or buy, there are also a few hire companies which allow their clients to reach a decision after they come back from holiday: if you hire a tent from them in order to try it out, and then decide to buy it (or a new version of the same model) on your return, they will waive the hire charge and allow you to pay just the purchase price of the tent.

Frame tents are usually supplied in two large sacks, or valises, one containing the collapsible tubular frame and the other holding the outer canvas plus the inner sleeping compartments. There is also a smaller bag containing the tent pegs and guy lines. Together they make up a weight of between 25 and 45 kg (55–100 lb) for a typical four-person tent, which is far too much to carry on a walking holiday! For holidays other than by car there are different, lighter kinds of tent (see page 39) but frame tents are generally much more convenient to live in. They are easy to erect, tall enough to stand upright in and spacious enough to contain separate sleeping and living areas.

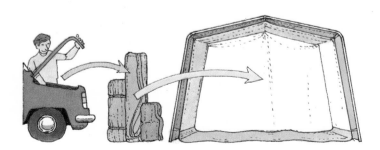

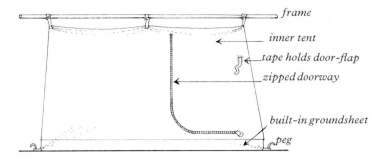

A question of size

Apart from the windows, the outer covering of frame tents is almost always made of canvas, with the roof of a slightly heavier grade than the walls. This traditional material is better than totally air- and watertight fabrics such as nylon and rubberised cloth because it 'breathes' and causes fewer condensation problems inside the tent. It does however have the peculiar property that while it is totally waterproof under normal circumstances, if you rub against it when the outside is wet from rain or dew, the wetness will begin to soak through.

Some allowance needs to be made for this when deciding on the size of tent that you are going to buy. Remember that the walls of virtually all frame tents slope inwards towards the roof and that the area at shoulder height is somewhat smaller than is suggested by the manufacturer's ground plan. For families with growing children, if the living space is too cramped, it becomes difficult to avoid brushing against the canvas during bad weather and water may then start to trickle down the inside of the tent wall.

For the same reason, frame tents are always designed to leave a gap between the outer walls and the inner sleeping compartments which hang from the frame and are usually made of thinner, non-waterproof cotton. Trouble can result if the inner cloth makes contact with the outer one, so again when choosing a tent you need to check that the sleeping compartments are actually large enough to take your beds or mattresses without being stretched outwards. Each sleeping compartment should have a sewn-in groundsheet which continues a few centimetres up the sides so as to form a waterproof tray. If the tray is too small, the mattresses will overlap and cause the non-waterproof cotton to make contact with the ground, and this too can lead to a spread of dampness.

Groundsheets and awnings

Outside the zipped doorway of the sleeping compartment, a groundsheet for the living area is also very worthwhile, although it frequently has to be bought as an extra. On a grassy site it may only be necessary to have a small mat as a place for removing grimy footwear before stepping into the sleeping compartment but in dusty or wet conditions bare earth can be very unpleasant and a larger area needs to be covered by the groundsheet in order to prevent dirt being transferred to the mattresses and bedding.

On the less gloomy side, with any luck your summer holidays will be warm and sunny, so staying dry will be less of a problem than keeping cool. The popularity of camping nowadays means that you may not be able to find a pitch that is shaded by trees, so you will probably wish to retreat into your tent for an occasional respite from the sun. Unfortunately, a closed-up tent often becomes stiflingly hot inside, rather like a car that has been left standing in the open, and to overcome this you will need a type with a wide doorway and openable window-flap in order to achieve good ventilation. Alternatively, some manufacturers either include a detachable awning with their models or offer one as an extra – though sometimes with a little ingenuity it is possible to obtain the same effect by unpegging one side of the tent and folding it back over the edge of the roof. Either way, this produces a shady place in which to relax.

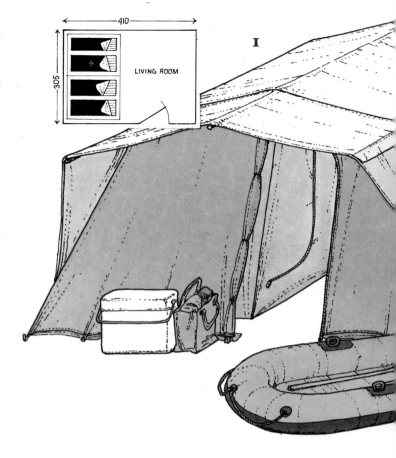

I *The basic family four: a popular and economical design which provides adequate sleeping accommodation but not much living area for use in wet weather. Weight approx. 27kg.*

2 *The combination frame and ridge tent: this design has the advantage that it has two separate sleeping compartments, which allows a degree of privacy, plus a living area that can be used fully because it occupies the highest part of the tent. Weight approx. 34kg.*

3 *The family six: this design offers a large living area with windows made of strong PVC. There is also a kitchen bay and an external seating area shaded by an awning. Weight approx. 40kg.*

20

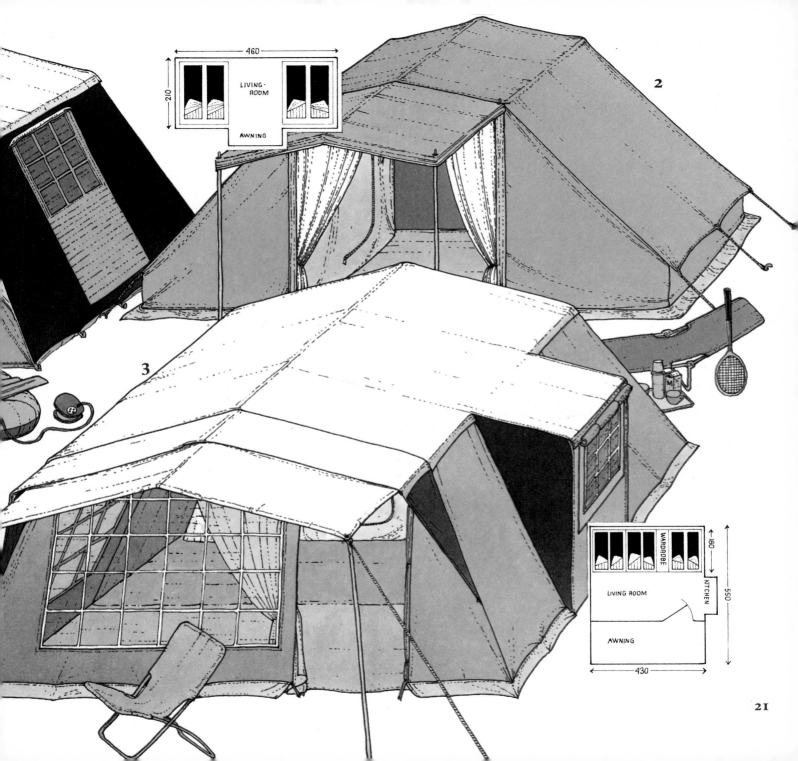

460

210

LIVING-
ROOM

AWNING

2

3

WARDROBE

180

LIVING ROOM

KITCHEN

550

AWNING

430

Putting the tent up

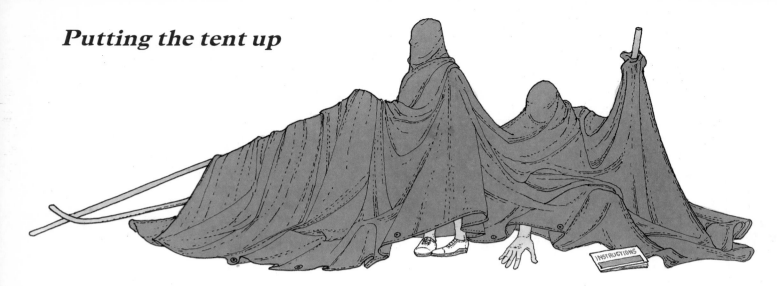

Pitching the tent for the first time is something that should ideally be done at home before the start of your holiday. It is not a difficult job but it does no harm to practise on a fine, calm day in the back garden so that the routine is already familiar by the time you arrive at the campsite. The steps involved are shown opposite and are roughly the same for all models. It is however a matter of choice whether, on dry days, you hang up the inner sleeping compartment first, before the outer canvas is spread, or leave it until the last. In rainy weather it should·be left until last so that it stays dry.

The tubular sections of the tent frame may all look confusingly similar when they are first tipped out of their separate bag, but you will usually find that the joints that make up the four corners of the roof are spring-linked to the sections which push into them. This makes it almost impossible to go wrong when fitting the pieces together. If they are not linked in this way, it is a good idea, once the frame is up, to mark the tubes to show which part fits into which. This can be done either with paint of different colours or by filing code marks into the metal.

With its sides securely pegged down, a well-designed frame tent is normally quite stable, so guy-lines need only be attached when strong winds are expected or if extra tethering is advisable in loose soil. During the daytime on the campsite there will be more danger of tripping over extended guy-lines than of having the tent blown over without warning, so the best plan is just to practise attaching the guy-lines to the rings at the corners of the roof canvas and then keep them in untangled loops ready for action if a storm does blow up.

1 *Assemble the top part of the frame on the ground and place it in the position where the tent is going to stand.*
2 *Add the legs of the frame with their 'knees' bent.*
3 *Unroll the canvas and hang it like a length of wallpaper over the three roof struts.*
4 *Straighten the legs, one pair at a time, to full height and half-peg the feet (see inset).*
5 *Hang the inner sleeping compartment from the top frame and peg down its built-in groundsheet, if necessary adjusting the slope of the legs to tauten or slacken the walls. When the feet are in their final position, peg them down fully.*
6 *Unfold the outer canvas, insert any awning supports and, with all zips closed, peg down the neoprene tent bands all round ensuring that only the waterproof skirt comes into contact with the ground (see insert showing correct 90° angle of a peg and the correct hang of a corner of the skirt).*

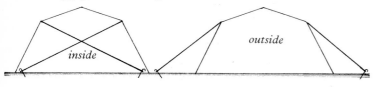

inside   *outside*

Taking it down again

When you are taking the tent down again, the erecting procedure is simply reversed, except that any soiled parts of the waterproof skirt should be sponged and allowed to dry before the canvas is rolled up. If for any reason the tent has to be packed up while it is still damp – for instance in wet weather or before the dew has evaporated in the early morning – it is absolutely essential to spread it out again for drying within a day or so. If care is not taken in this respect, the fabric can become mildewed and discoloured, or in extreme cases weakened by rot.

During the practice in the garden, you should not have to deal with a wet tent, so concentrate on packing it together neatly in preparation for the holiday. The canvas should be folded so that a door or window is visible on the outside of the bundle, then you will be able to see which way round to lift it onto the frame. This is also a good opportunity for repacking the valise containing the canvas in such a way that it suits the allotted space in your car. The tent can be made into a long thin roll or a short fat one, or even folded square if that is more convenient.

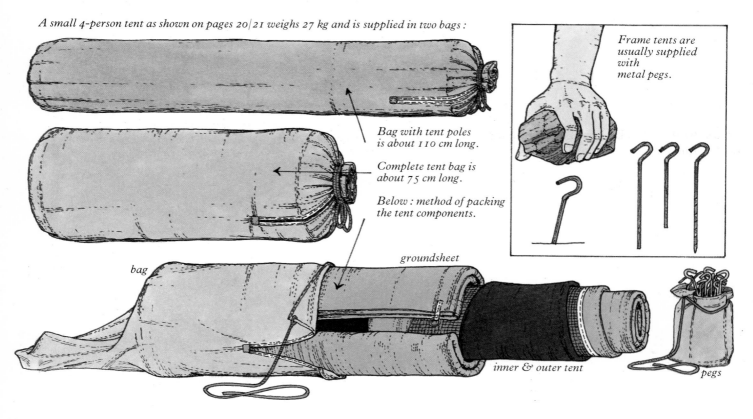

A small 4-person tent as shown on pages 20/21 weighs 27 kg and is supplied in two bags :

Frame tents are usually supplied with metal pegs.

Bag with tent poles is about 110 cm long.

Complete tent bag is about 75 cm long.

Below : method of packing the tent components.

bag   *groundsheet*   *inner & outer tent*   *pegs*

Equipping the camp kitchen

If you take a look around your well-equipped kitchen at home, with its plumbed-in sink, its spacious oven, its four-ring hob, its refrigerator, dishwasher, electric food-mixer and so on, it is fairly clear that no portable camp kitchen is likely to match up to it for sheer convenience and labour-saving efficiency. It follows, therefore, that when you go camping you should not expect to cook and eat as elaborately as at home.

To cook or not to cook

One way to approach the question of food, in fact, is to budget fairly generously and to take the family to a restaurant for one main meal every day throughout the holiday. This naturally costs more than preparing each meal yourselves, but since you have saved money on overnight accommodation you may feel that you can afford to spend a little extra on keeping yourselves well fed. Many of the larger campsites have their own restaurant, which is very convenient. Or if you happen to be staying in an area that is famous for its local dishes, sampling the menu at the local *tavernas* or *Gaststätten* can become one of the major pleasures of the holiday.

Choosing and using a stove

Even if you decide to keep the amount of cooking to a minimum, however, you will still need to take along a stove of some kind. The most practical types are the ones which run off pressurised cartridges of gas or, for a larger family, refillable cylinders. A selection of models is shown below. Wherever you spend your holiday, there is little danger of running out of fuel with these stoves because you can tell by shaking the cartridge or cylinder how much liquified gas there is left. Virtually every campsite shop stocks replacements at fairly standard prices, so that all you have to do is to buy a new one on the spot: it is hardly worthwhile to take a spare with you from home.

A   Picnic stove takes a standard small gas cartridge which is obtainable virtually everywhere. Stabilisers help to prevent it from falling over during cooking.
B   Single burner stove with piezo-electric ignition – helpful if you can never find the matches!
C   Double burner lightweight model which runs off a larger gas canister with the aid of a low-pressure regulator.
D   Super Grillogaz double burner and grill. A high-speed stove equipped with a grill, which also packs flat for carrying.

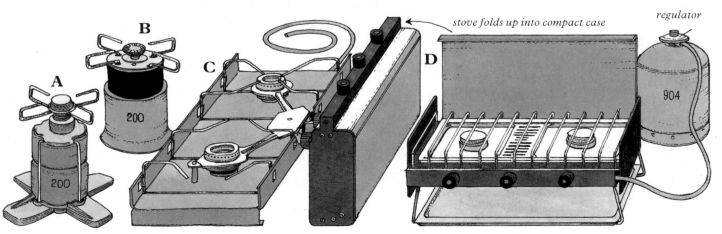

stove folds up into compact case · regulator

25

For cooking operations, usually the stove is placed either on the ground or on the same folding table at which you are going to take your meals. But if this seems too makeshift, and if you have enough space in the car, it is possible to purchase the type of purpose-built lightweight stand shown in the illustration on the right. It is as well to remember, though, that cooking inside the tent on a stand that raises the stove very near to the roof or walls can be a hazardous business. In well-designed tents, and with a stand that has a metal surround, the canvas is protected from being splashed or catching fire. But if you are in any doubt it is better to avoid danger and cook outside, employing a windshield to conserve the stove's heat.

Other useful equipment
This matter of heat loss is the chief drawback of camp cooking. Food takes longer to warm up and cools very quickly in the open air, so there is no doubt that two burners are better than one for ensuring that all parts of a meal start off hot simultaneously.

With a single burner, some additional equipment helps to overcome the disadvantage. For example, a couple of screw-top vacuum flasks enable hot water, coffee or soup to be prepared in advance and kept warm. A wide-mouthed vacuum jar enables the same to be done with, say, vegetables accompanying a meat dish; and of course all saucepans should have well-fitting lids to stop heat escaping.

Another useful accessory is a small portable immersion heater of the type that can be bought in its own plastic pouch. Where permissible, this can be plugged into a socket in the campsite's washing or ironing room and will heat up a panful of water more quickly than a picnic stove, saving on bottled gas at the same time.

A good can-opener is essential, of course, plus a bottle-opener, corkscrew, breadknife and serving spoon. Saucepans, kettles, egg-poachers, frying pans etc. can be the ordinary household ones from home provided that they are not *too* heavy, but with a frying pan it is sometimes difficult to clean out the fat after every meal under camping conditions, so it too should have a lid.

A set of plastic food containers with airtight lids is also desirable for storing items of food. They can be placed in a bucket of water or in a stream to keep such things as butter cool. Alternatively, a substitute for a refrigerator is an insulated container such as the one illustrated opposite. It can be kept cool with an ice pack or freezing sachet, or by putting into it a packet of frozen food which will keep the interior chilled as it gradually thaws.

Cooking table with windshield. Including the cooker, it folds up into a neat case 22 × 60 × 32 cm (shown below).

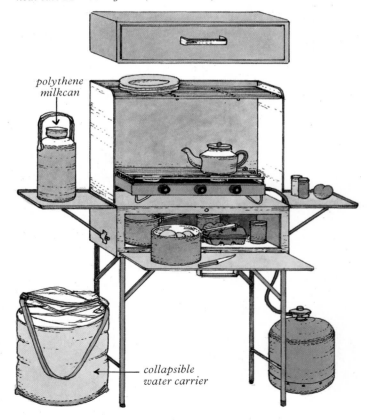

polythene milkcan

collapsible water carrier

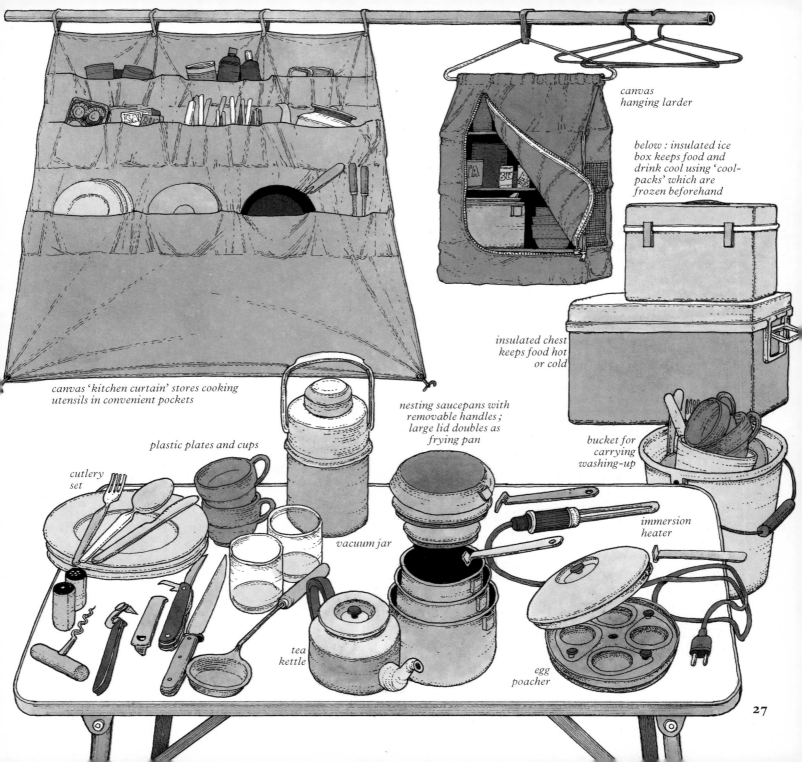

canvas hanging larder

below: insulated ice box keeps food and drink cool using 'cool-packs' which are frozen beforehand

insulated chest keeps food hot or cold

bucket for carrying washing-up

immersion heater

canvas 'kitchen curtain' stores cooking utensils in convenient pockets

nesting saucepans with removable handles; large lid doubles as frying pan

plastic plates and cups

cutlery set

vacuum jar

tea kettle

egg poacher

27

A barbecue feast

Perhaps rather more appropriate than a frying pan for outdoor cooking is a portable barbecue or hibachi. On organised campsites or indeed anywhere in the countryside where fire could spread, traditional camp fires are not permitted, but a safely constructed barbecue which burns small pieces of charcoal is much more acceptable. Charcoal-grilled steaks, sausages or fish make a delicious feast when served in the open with salads and hunks of bread, and the shimmering heat of the barbecue is almost as heartwarming as a genuine campfire.

Tackling the washing up

Following each meal, there is the regular chore of washing up but this is not a problem if all members of the family, including the youngest ones, can take turns at the job. All good campsites have a set of large kitchen sinks where hot water is on tap, either free of charge or via a coin-in-the-slot meter, so it will simply be a matter of carrying all the utensils there and back from the place where your tent is pitched.

For this purpose, one or two plastic buckets are more practical than a washing up bowl: crockery can be placed in them and carried with one hand whereas a bowl takes two hands and may be difficult for a small child to balance. Having all your crockery made of chip-proof plastic also helps to make fetching and carrying safer. The washing up liquid fits into the bucket too if it is in a small container; so does a plastic foam pad that has a scouring side to cope with the cleaning of pans.

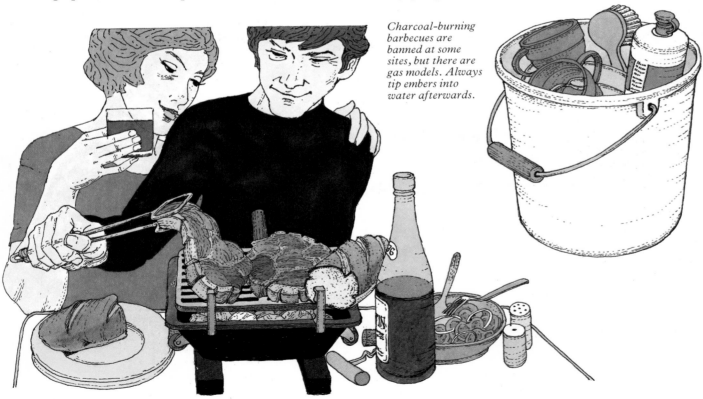

Charcoal-burning barbecues are banned at some sites, but there are gas models. Always tip embers into water afterwards.

28

Apart from making sure that it is not easily breakable, there are no special requirements when selecting crockery and cutlery for camping. Naturally, it does not make sense to take along the family's Dresden china or parts of a complete dinner set which would be ruined if one piece went missing. But the other extreme of using only disposable plastic knives, forks and spoons is also not the answer: they seem to make even substantial food taste like an airline snack. The best compromise is perhaps low-priced stainless steel cutlery, and it should be packed as far as possible in a way that does not allow it to rattle in the car. The corkscrew and any sharp-pointed knife should have an old cork stuck on the end.

If you are visiting a winegrowing region, you will almost certainly want to enjoy a bottle or two of the local vintage with your meals or in the mellow hours of a warm summer evening. It is worth packing a few genuine glasses for this purpose since it rather spoils the pleasure to have to drink wine out of plastic tumblers, and it certainly inhibits you from inviting the charming couple on the next pitch over to join you.

Camping tables, chairs and stools are rather leggy things and always seem to stick out when you are trying to close the lid of the boot. Nevertheless, they make life on the campsite much more comfortable than always having to picnic on the ground. The ones below on this page are made of strong lightweight metal and fold more or less flat, and the table has a wipe-clean, heat-resistant top.

The air mattresses and campbeds that are used for sleeping at night make excellent places to recline during the day so long as they can be kept reasonably clean; a sunshade and/or a windbreak are worthwhile for keeping off the scorching sun and sea breezes.

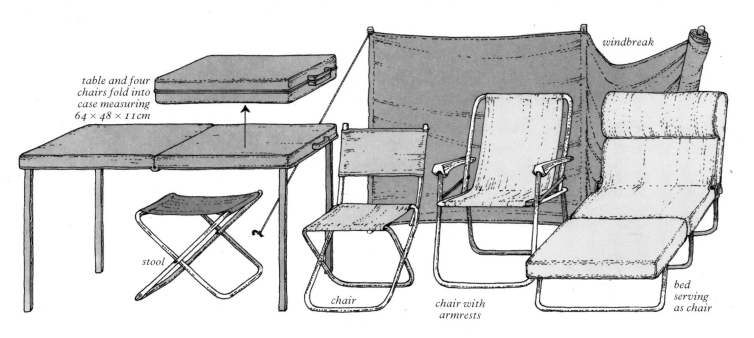

table and four chairs fold into case measuring 64 × 48 × 11 cm

windbreak

stool

chair

chair with armrests

bed serving as chair

Selecting a site

In a few of the less densely populated countries including Norway, Sweden and Finland there is no law against camping for a short time in the publicly-owned countryside, apart from in certain restricted areas. In other countries, subject to local byelaws, farmers can give permission for you to put up a tent on their private land. But for the most part, ordinary holidaymakers prefer to stay at organised campsites. The advantage of doing so is that a number of important facilities are always provided: a drinking water supply, clean toilets and washrooms, proper garbage disposal and electricity for such things as shavers. Often too there are additional amenities such as a shop, a restaurant, a children's playground and a public callbox.

Security is ensured to some extent by the fact that site wardens require proof of identity and in some cases actually retain visitors' passports during their stay. A number of sites in mainland Europe are also open only to holders of an International Camping Carnet which has to be obtained from a camping or motoring organisation before you set off from home; that too discourages the sort of visitor who is likely to act unsociably, as do the charges which the site makes for each overnight stay. The 'Carnet' is a worthwhile thing to have when you are touring as it incorporates third party insurance while you are staying at a site and occasionally entitles you to reduced prices.

It is not possible to give a precise indication here of the cost of staying at a campsite. The charges vary from site to site and from year to year. But they are generally made up of separate small sums: a charge for the car, a charge for the tent, a charge for each adult and a charge for each child. This all adds up to more than at first appears, but as has been said before, it is still cheap compared with the cost of hotel accommodation.

This is not the place either in which to recommend individual campsites. The authors once had the disconcerting experience of going back to a peaceful, idyllic site beside a beautiful lake in Sweden and finding that its character had changed completely since their previous visit. It was full to bursting point. The explanation turned out to be that a trailblazing German tourist had likewise discovered this quiet spot and in his enthusiasm had published an account of its charms in a popular camping magazine. Of course from that time on the site remained just as beautiful, but it could no longer be enjoyed for its quietness!

Consulting a guide

If you have personal friends who have been camping for several years, you may be lucky enough to prize out of them the location of their favourite site. But you should also buy one of the excellent guides to campsites that are on the market, preferably one that is available to members of a camping club or some other organisation which assesses the merits of the sites it lists. From the maps that the guide contains, you will be able to select an area where there are several sites within easy distance of each other. The close grouping probably indicates that the area is an attractive one for visitors, and the facilities should be good since the sites are competing with each other for custom. It should also mean that you can be certain of finding a pitch at one or other of the places shown. Beware, however, of sites that are grouped around ferry-crossing points: they may be perfectly pleasant places but they are so convenient for people coming off the boat late at night or departing early in the morning that the atmosphere tends to be rather restless for a longer stay.

Interpreting the hieroglyphs
The guide will tell you briefly how to find each site and then show by means of symbols what facilities it offers. A typical entry and how to interpret it is shown here:

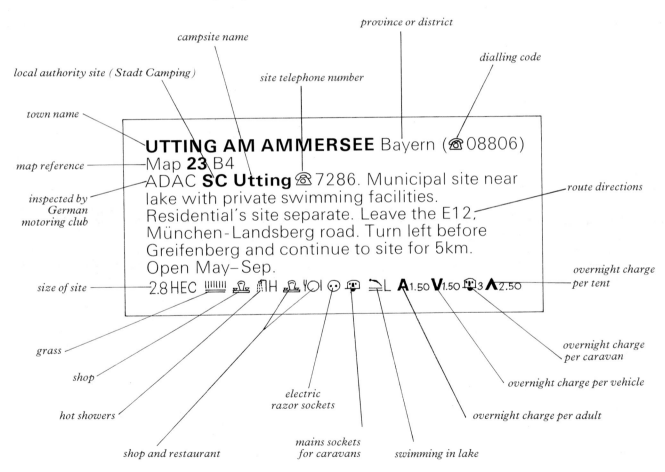

The perils of the one night stand

Putting up and taking down the tent, inflating and deflating several air mattresses, unpacking and repacking the car; all this is a fairly strenuous business until it has become absolutely routine and each member of the family knows exactly what to do. So try to avoid having a hurried overnight stop as your first experience of camping.

On the outward journey, if the holiday area you have chosen is more than an easy day's drive away from home and you want to camp for a single night on the way, try to divide up the distance so that you arrive early at the first, intermediate site and leave fairly late the following morning. Alternatively, it might be better to stop off for bed and breakfast at a small hotel. Later on, you may be proud of your quick getaway techniques or your ability to put up the tent in the dark; but arriving on an unfamiliar pitch at midnight and departing at dawn is not the happiest way for first-time campers to lose their innocence!

The perfect pitch

On arrival at the campsite you will probably see a notice requesting all visitors to check in at the reception counter straight away. Experienced campers never do so. They park the car somewhere near the entrance, everyone climbs out and then they take a good look around the site.

Just like hotel guests in the old days who would never dream of accepting a room before they were shown what was being offered to them, you should make a quick inspection tour of the facilities before definitely deciding to stay. This is one of the great privileges of a camping holiday. You can check the cleanliness of the toilets, see whether there is hot water on tap, work out the overnight charges and, above all, make sure that there is a good pitch available.

Easy access

Ideas about what constitutes a good pitch may vary, but there are several points to be taken into consideration. The first one is access. Since you are now inspecting the site on foot, do not forget that you will need to bring the car up close to where the tent is going to be pitched and preferably be able to leave it there afterwards. The car contains all your equipment and is your only lockable storage cupboard for items that might be worth stealing. As long as it is near at hand, miscellaneous belongings can be kept in it and the tent will not be too cluttered. You may also wish to run an inflator or a lamp off its battery, to sit in it and listen to the radio or simply to have it in a position where you can keep an eye on it. To enable you to do all this, the pitch, however attractive it looks, will be unsuitable if it is a long way from any access road and is cut off by rocks or marshy ground. However, it is not a good idea to be either too near to, or too far away from, the central block of toilets and washrooms. If you camp too near to them, people making a beeline for the facilities will be cutting across your pitch at all hours of the day and night and you will be disturbed all the time by a background of clatter and chatter. Too far away, on the other hand, and the route march becomes inconvenient every time you run short of drinking water or try to persuade the children that they should go and wash their hands.

On large sites, the area nearest to the service block is sometimes reserved for caravans so that they can be connected to the mains electricity supply, and in this case there is no option but to pitch the tent further away. Often, though, there are supplementary water taps and small lavatories near the edges of the site to reduce the amount of to-ing and fro-ing.

No two campsites are exactly the same and choosing a pitch becomes an entertaining task in which each member of the family can have a vote. At Morteratsch near Pontresina in Switzerland, the municipal campsite rambles over an area of about a square kilometre, interspersed with trees and scrub and a number of rushing glacial streams. There is a choice between a few sheltered pitches and others on open, boulder-strewn ground that have a view of snow-capped mountains. Or if younger opinions prevail, you may find yourselves marooned between milky streams on a low mini-desert island, wondering whether the louder sounds at night mean that the waters on the other side of the canvas have suddenly begun to rise. In contrast, many sites beside the endless beaches along the west coast of Denmark are small and functional, divided into numbered pitches by chest-high hedges. Here it is a matter of selecting a number and moving into your chosen accommodation as if it were a kind of unfurnished outdoor apartment.

MORTERATSCH Graubünden (☎ 082) Map **12** B3. **Plauns** ☎ 66285. On Pontresina-Bernina Road. 0.4HEC ⟪⟫ ⦂• ◈ 🅼H ☉ 🐟 🎏 🅱 ⚠ ⊞ lau ⟼ 🍴 ⦿ ⵡ

Below : view of the campsite at Morteratsch.

33

Advantages and drawbacks

The hedges on the Danish sites are a means of providing a reasonable amount of privacy between one pitch and the next. When there are no hedges, you will want to make sure that your tent is at least ten metres from the neighbouring one, preferably more, because tent walls are thin and do little to muffle intimate conversations.

Ideally, the pitch should be absolutely flat, although a slight slope does not matter as long as things can be arranged so that it runs downwards towards the foot end of the sleeping compartment. Sleeping with your feet uphill can be uncomfortable since any slipping movement tends to press your head up against the canvas wall. Avoid pitches that have a dip in the middle because if it rains heavily, water will run inwards and you may find yourselves the proud owners of a tent with its own indoor swimming pool!

Other unforeseen snags can generally be avoided by first-time campers, if they are in any doubt, by moving onto a pitch that shows signs of having been much used before. Favourite spots are ones that receive the sun in the morning and the evening but are shaded by trees from its full mid-day heat. Camping right under a tree has its drawbacks, however. The roots tend to make the ground uneven and for some time after rain, the tent may be bombarded by large, sticky droplets. Falling berries can stain the canvas and at night the slightest breeze sounds like a hurricane that is about to bring branches down on top of you.

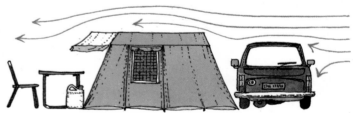

Sometimes the best form of shelter is a wall or line of bushes on the windward side. Any windbreak at all is better than being completely in the open, so if the site is totally exposed, try to park the car on the side of the tent from which the prevailing wind blows. Finally, a space in front of the tent where you can sit and lie is absolutely essential.

Once the pitch has been cleared of sharp, groundsheet-piercing debris such as small stones, twigs and pine cones, the tent can be erected and the family can move into its new canvas home. This is an exciting occasion so there should be no shortage of willing hands to unload the bedding, chairs etc. from the car and make everything shipshape for the night.

If you have managed to arrive early at the site, there may still be time to spare for an exploratory walk when everything is done – down to the nearby beach or into the local village. Otherwise if it is already evening and everyone is hungry from the journey, it may be best to prepare a meal straight away. Except perhaps in hotter countries, the pleasantest time to eat supper out of doors is before the sun has quite disappeared, while there is still time to linger over coffee after the meal without feeling chilly or being overtaken by the dark.

If alternatively you decide to leave the site and go out by car for a meal, it is a good idea to make all the bedtime preparations in advance. It is possible to take towels and toothbrushes with you, then if you find it is after 11 pm when you return, you will be able to park the car near the service block, wash and get ready for bed and then make your way quietly back to the tent together on foot. This avoids any disturbance which might be caused by driving back to your pitch past people who have gone to bed early, and of course the car can easily be retrieved in the morning.

Lamps and torches
Around the entrance to the service block, lights often stay on automatically until after midnight, but further away it really does become pitch dark on most campsites at night and some form of tent lighting is a necessity. Candles and Chinese lanterns can be quite effective in sheltered corners *outside* the tent but they should never be relied upon for providing light *inside*.

The risk of setting the canvas alight makes them literally not worth the candle!

There are several much safer and more powerful types of lantern which run off gas cartridges, the car battery or their own replaceable dry cells (see illustration). The choice here is a personal one and as usual may depend on which type is most useful to you during the rest of the year when you are not on holiday. Since batteries and gas cartridges all have a limited life, however, it is cheaper to finish any camp chores before nightfall and not to sit up reading into the early hours.

Incidentally, anyone who has walked through a campsite after dark will be aware that if a lantern is placed low down inside a tent it acts as a point source and produces the most entertaining shadow-play on the canvas walls. For people who are sensitive about projecting their silhouettes while undressing, for the benefit of passers-by, the solution is to hang the lamp high up from the central strut of the tent frame or simply switch it off altogether.

In addition to the main lantern, it is also advisable to take along at least one pocket torch for each sleeping compartment in the tent. Then any member of the family who needs to make his way to the toilets during the night can do so without getting lost. Young children also feel more secure if they have a light ready to hand, though they need to be warned against leaving it on when they fall asleep.

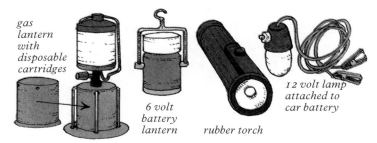

gas lantern with disposable cartridges

6 volt battery lantern

rubber torch

12 volt lamp attached to car battery

Precautions before retiring

The torch inside the sleeping compartment also serves for a last-minute check, when everyone is bedded down, to ensure that no insects have found their way inside the inner tent lining. Midges can sometimes be troublesome to city-dwellers with tender skins, especially on campsites near rivers and lakes, but once inside the zipped-up sleeping compartment they are usually safe from them thanks to the fine mesh from which ventilation panels are made. It is only a matter of remembering to dispose of any that have already intruded.

For campers there are several other routine jobs before retiring to bed which are the equivalent of bolting the door and closing the shutters at home. Apart from seeing that the car is safely locked and filling the vacuum flask ready for morning tea in bed, most of these precautions are against a possible worsening of the weather. In summertime it is not very likely that any disaster will strike but, as mentioned before, even light winds and gentle showers tend to sound like storm conditions in the silence of the night, so a few elementary steps will save you from lying awake and worrying about whether all is secure.

Guarding against wind and rain
Perhaps the first thing to do is to make sure that no possessions are left outside where they may get wet or be blown away. Towels and swimming costumes that have been hung out to dry should be brought into the tent; so should camping chairs and tables and they should be arranged so that none of them touches the inside of the canvas where it might cause water to seep through. Window flaps should be closed and doors zipped up and no gaps should be left around the skirting of the tent where wind and rain could penetrate. It sometimes helps in this respect if the groundsheet is arranged so that its edges are turned up a few centimetres, overlapping the inside of the skirting.

In very wet conditions, channels can be dug in the soil around the tent to carry the rainwater away and prevent it from running inside. A small collapsible-handled spade or a garden trowel is useful for this purpose. But channelling spoils the pitch for the next occupiers if their tent is larger than yours, so it should only be dug as an emergency measure and then refilled afterwards. Indeed on some sites it is actually banned.

Prolonged heavy rain can lead to unpleasant sogginess underfoot but it does not present any actual danger. The roof and walls of a modern tent are designed to withstand it. Wind on the other hand can be a vicious enemy to holiday campers because of the sheer area of material contained in a frame tent. The same size of sailcloth enables a stiff breeze to drive a small boat along at over 20 knots, so naturally if the wind penetrates underneath a poorly tethered tent it can generate enough force to buckle the frame and carry the canvas off to Munchkinland.

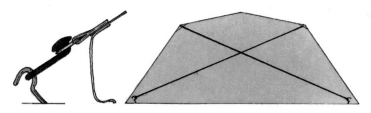

The best safeguard against this is to do a quick round of the tentpegs each evening and check that they are securely in position at roughly 90° to the slope of the tent walls. A few spare pegs, preferably large wooden ones, should always be carried so that the anchorage can be doubled up in sandy soil. Then if there are any signs of a blustery night to come, guy-lines should be fixed to the special lugs on the top outside corners, secured either to the ground or to a convenient tree. Alternatively, the last person to go to bed can fasten diagonal lines from the ground to a couple of the angles *inside* the tent: the geometry of frame tents makes these internal guy-lines – or the special storm poles that are available – particularly efficient.

Beating an emergency retreat

Beginners should not worry unduly about disasters, though. In many years of camping, the authors have only once encountered wind conditions bad enough to justify taking down the tent in the middle of the night. This was at Odda in Norway where a narrowing, steep-sided valley helped to funnel an exceptional gale onto the municipal camping field. Although we were not very experienced campers at the time, we did the right thing which was to remove everything from inside the tent first, then collapse the frame *before* removing any of the surrounding pegs. If tentpegs are removed on the windward side while a frame tent is still standing, there is a high risk that the canvas will balloon out uncontrollably and tear.

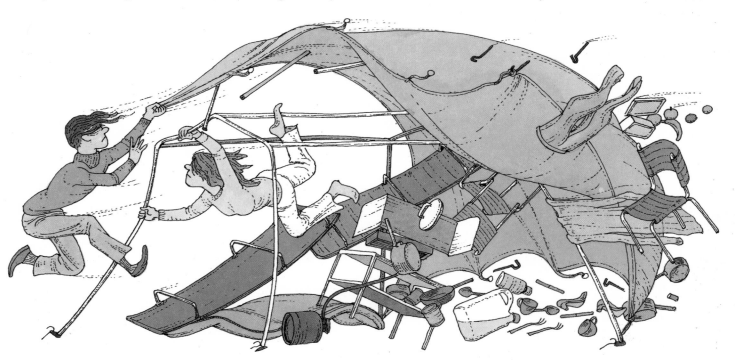

Lightweight camping

The taste of adventure

When travelling by car, a large family may have a little trouble stowing all its camping gear into the boot or tethering things onto the roof rack. But usually there is still room for one or two luxuries to be included and very few home comforts have to be sacrificed entirely. Space can generally be found for several changes of clothing; for bulky quilt-type sleeping bags; for chairs, stools, full-length mattresses and even for some of the ordinary, fairly heavy pots, pans and cutlery out of the home kitchen cupboard. Even the frame tent in which the family sleeps is quite generous in size. It is large and square and has all the characteristics of a small house, with ample headroom and separate living and sleeping compartments – by no means the minimum space that would be needed just for bedding down for the night.

For people travelling without a car, however, the situation is quite different. If you go camping on foot, by bike or in a canoe, the limitations on weight and space are much more severe. When all the essentials for living have to be crammed into a rucksack or a couple of cycle panniers, the concept of transporting a kind of miniature version of home has to be abandoned. In fact the holiday begins to demand certain sacrifices and requires more of the equipment to be purpose-built. It becomes a sporting adventure and takes on the special name of lightweight camping.

Thinking ahead

Most people who take up lightweight camping begin in their teens, most probably at the end of their schooldays and after they have already experienced camping in a frame tent along with parents or friends. This means that it is sensible for families with children to think ahead. If there is a son or daughter who is growing up and is likely to go off on an independent camping holiday before long, this future possibility should be allowed to influence the stock of camping gear that is built up over the years. For example, when someone in the family needs a new sleeping bag, it may be worthwhile to buy a lightweight one instead of a bulky quilt-type bag. Or when choosing a new or supplementary cooker, the family might settle for a light single-burner instead of a heavy two-burner stove. In this way, the newly-independent teenager will not suddenly find one summer that he has to buy all his lightweight equipment from scratch – an expensive business that may well deter him from camping altogether.

This policy of foresight sometimes even extends to the initial choice of tent for the family camping holidays. In some cases, instead of investing in one single large frame tent with accommodation for six people, it might be sensible to buy a four-berth frame tent plus a separate lightweight tent for use by two of the children. On a combined holiday, the smaller tent can be pitched alongside the larger one as a kind of dormitory annexe, but as soon as the children are old enough they can actually start to go off with the lightweight tent for a holiday by themselves.

Lightweight camping is also not only for the young. There is nothing to prevent a father from going off for a weekend's walking tour with his son and a small tent is also a very good standby if a couple is touring around by car and is occasionally unable to find bed-and-breakfast accommodation as planned.

One plus one equals one-and-a-half

Another advance consideration about lightweight camping is that if two people go on holiday together they can share certain items of equipment and so lighten the individual load that each of them has to carry. Or, seen from another point of view, between the two of them they can take along a few extra items.

For example, one person travelling alone would probably have to carry such things as a stove, a box of matches, cooking utensils, a torch or candle, a map and a compass. However, two people on holiday together would not need to duplicate any of these items. The same point applies if two friends are able to share a tent: a two-person tent is not likely to be twice as heavy as a one-person tent so again there is a net saving of weight.

For this practical reason, as well as for the companionship and security that is to be gained by holidaying with a friend, it is often a good idea to plan a lightweight camping holiday as a shared venture. If this is done right from the start, it not only influences the choice of equipment but also reduces the costs.

Paddling your own canoe

Clearly, one place where it is not wise to venture alone is onto a river or lake, but if you can swim and are used to the water, canoeing makes a delightful basis for a camping holiday. You can either set off to explore the waterways near home (and it is surprising how many discoveries you make when you see a familiar landscape from this new angle); or the canoes can be transported to your starting point on a roof rack or trailer.

In northern Germany, for example, there is an area known as the "Holstein Switzerland" around the town of Plön and it is easy to spend a fortnight here paddling around the inter-connecting lakes and staying at several established campsites. The authors also spent part of one holiday canoeing on the sea, in the sheltered waters among the skerries on the eastern coast of Sweden. There is nothing to compare with the sense of freedom accorded by this form of lightweight camping because with a small tent and an adequate supply of food you can actually spend the nights alone on your own wooded island, surrounded by the tideless ripples of the Baltic. The only wild animals against which any defence is needed are the restlessly scavenging ants!

In our own case, we were lucky enough to be able to borrow a couple of excellent German folding canoes which would fit into a large car boot. But in some places canoes or small boats can be hired on the spot, complete with lifejackets and one or two other items of equipment.

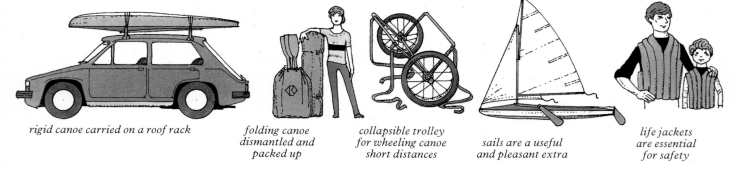

rigid canoe carried on a roof rack   *folding canoe dismantled and packed up*   *collapsible trolley for wheeling canoe short distances*   *sails are a useful and pleasant extra*   *life jackets are essential for safety*

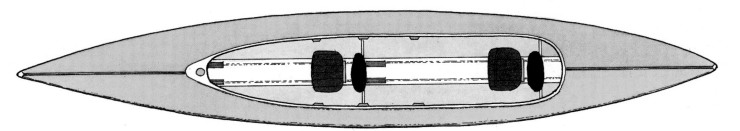

Above : a rigid canoe is suitable for camping but it is bulky to transport. When not in use, it requires storage space such as a shed, or it can be hung in slings under a garage ceiling.

Below : a folding canoe can be taken out of its bags and assembled in 30 minutes. Dismantled, it occupies much less space and can be carried inside a car or stored in a garage corner.

Bottom : equipment (shown packed in watertight bags) for two people camping by canoe.

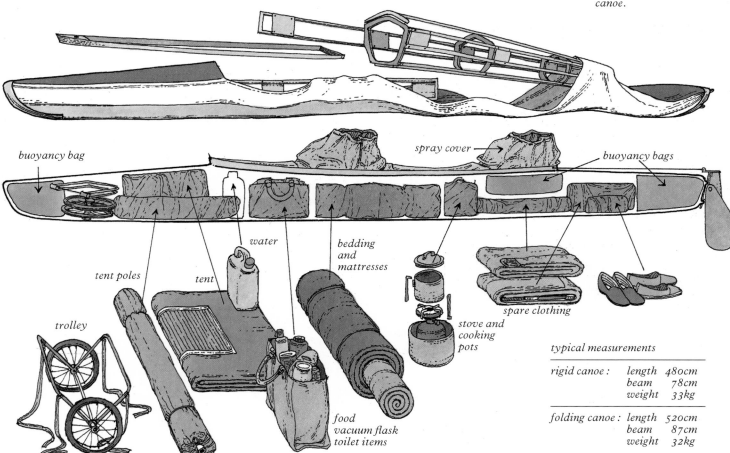

buoyancy bag

spray cover

buoyancy bags

water

bedding and mattresses

tent poles

tent

spare clothing

trolley

stove and cooking pots

food
vacuum flask
toilet items

typical measurements

rigid canoe :	length	480cm
	beam	78cm
	weight	33kg
folding canoe :	length	520cm
	beam	87cm
	weight	32kg

Camping by bike

More commonly, many people have their own bicycle and by undertaking a lightweight camping tour at Easter or midsummer can explore further afield than on individual day trips. On such tours it is not sensible to carry anything on your back while cycling – why burden yourself with the weight and make yourself dangerously top heavy? Instead, special panniers are slung over a light frame so that they hang on either side of the back wheel to the rear of the saddle. There is also room for a third container or a rolled-up tent on top of the frame. In addition, it is sometimes possible to fit smaller panniers over the front wheel but care should be taken not to make the bike too heavy at the front. This may affect the steering and make the machine very difficult to handle on slippery bends.

For touring with a fully loaded bicycle, it is of course helpful for the machine to have a gear-selector to ease you over the hills. The brakes must be capable of holding back the extra weight on steep descents. For lighting, a dynamo is more economical than battery-powered lamps, although a detachable front lamp powered by built-in batteries can double as a torch in emergencies.

Only one bicycle pump, one repair kit and one spare inner tube need be carried between two or three cyclists but you will each require a separate padlock and chain for parking the bike securely and a portable sack for taking snacks, rainwear and valuables with you whenever you are sightseeing on foot. Finally, if you are going abroad where traffic uses the opposite side of the road, practise pushing the bike and mounting and dismounting on the "wrong" side. This is difficult to do at first, especially with a loaded machine that is more wobbly than usual.

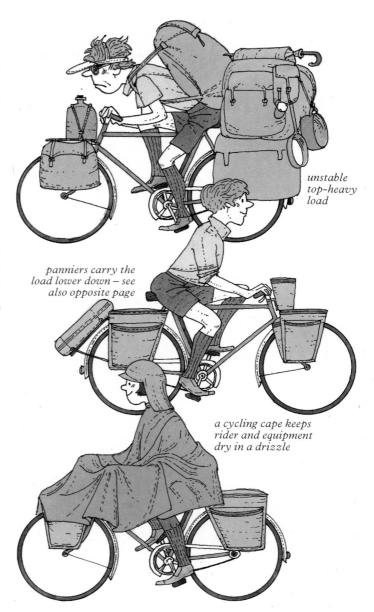

unstable top-heavy load

panniers carry the load lower down – see also opposite page

a cycling cape keeps rider and equipment dry in a drizzle

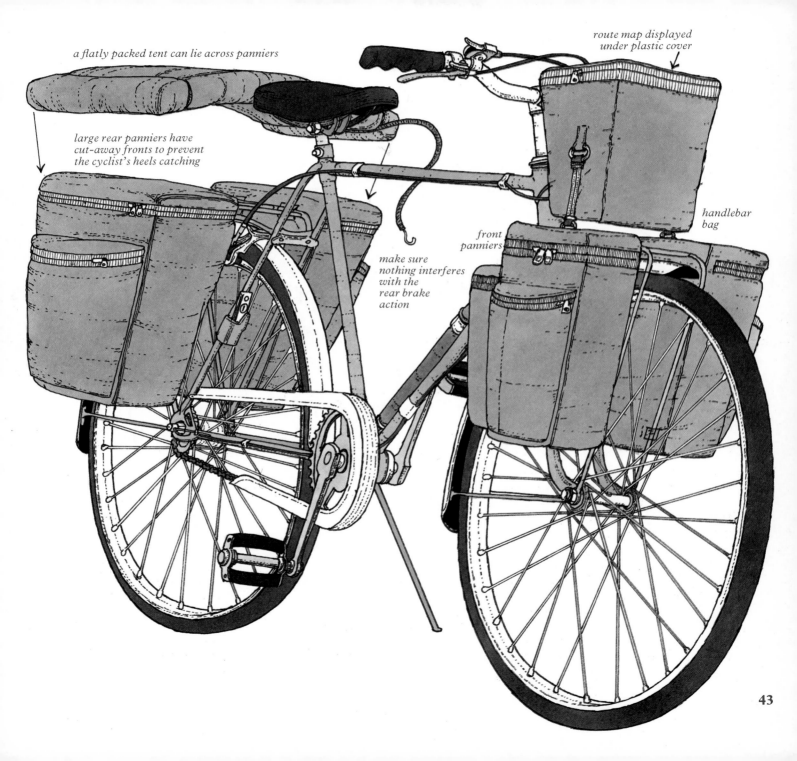

a flatly packed tent can lie across panniers

large rear panniers have cut-away fronts to prevent the cyclist's heels catching

route map displayed under plastic cover

handlebar bag

front panniers

make sure nothing interferes with the rear brake action

43

Motorcycling for two

In some ways, two people touring on a single motorcycle are subject to greater packing restrictions than a pair of cyclists on push-bikes. Weight is not such a problem because the engine will take the strain, but there is only a limited amount of space for two people's gear, especially inside hard, streamlined panniers which do not expand. Motorcyclists also have to cope with much bulkier protective clothing than ordinary cyclists.

The consequence is that if you are intending to take a camping holiday by motorcycle, you should not be misled by the cubic capacity of the engine: it is the cubic capacity of the panniers on the back of the pillion that counts. So you should choose equipment that packs up small – nesting pans and cutlery, a tent with short nesting poles, a compact stove that folds into a neat box, high quality, compressible down-filled sleeping bags etc. On the whole it is also better to stay at official campsites rather than camp "wild". In that way, for sightseeing daytrips or an afternoon on the beach you can leave the tent where it stands together with anything else that might perhaps attract thieves if it were left invitingly strapped onto your parked machine.

Holidaying on foot and carrying all your worldly goods in a rucksack is known as backpacking. Twenty-five years ago, a student could hoist his bulging pack onto his shoulders, walk cheerfully out of his mother's front door and be a thousand kilometres away by the following evening without having spent a penny on transport. But that was in the days when hitchhiking was still pursued in a friendly spirit, before its image was tarnished and it became associated with robbery and sexual attacks. There is still nothing wrong with hitchhiking at least ninety-nine times out of a hundred but it is the risk of an unpleasant experience on the hundredth occasion that has spoilt the idea of a hitchhiking holiday for many young people. It has also given them the perfect excuse for begging the cost of a coach, rail or air ticket off their worried parents!

Nowadays, the fashionable thing is to buy an international railcard of the type that gives you a month's go-as-you-please travel over the whole of the European rail network and to take in, say, a visit to the Parthenon, a week in the Austrian Alps and a glimpse of the midnight sun in Lapland. On this sort of holiday the distances covered are immense, especially since there is a tendency at first to make savings on accommodation and travelling time by sleeping on longdistance night trains.

But soon the novelty of waking up in a different country each morning begins to wear off. It is replaced by a yearning to stretch the legs, get off the beaten railway track and see what the greener parts of the world are like beyond the noisy concrete platform and the bustling station forecourt.

This is when lightweight camping equipment and a good, detailed map come into their own and really make it possible to enjoy being completely footloose and fancy free.

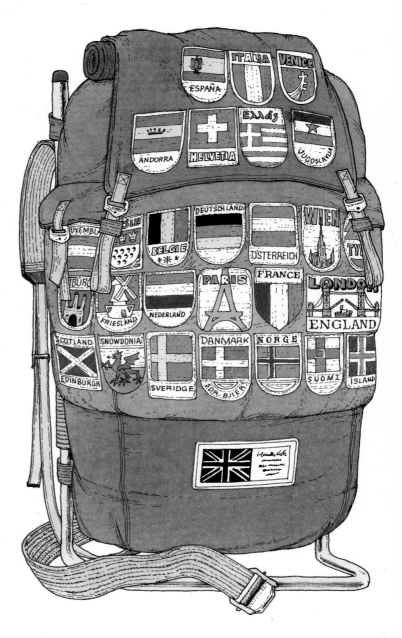

What to carry and how far to carry it

Unless you are the sort of person who thrives on assault courses and marathon runs, carrying a loaded rucksack all day long or cycling uphill with heavy panniers is quite strenuous exercise. It therefore makes sense to get yourself reasonably fit before you set out on holiday and to experiment with carrying different loads over a period of several hours. Aching muscles are to be expected in the first few days of a walking or cycling tour however little you carry: you will not yet be fully in trim. But at the end of the holiday you want to be in the happy situation of not even noticing the weight on your back – not worn out and returning home in need of another fortnight's rest.

Various formulae have been suggested for how much a backpacker should carry. One popular idea is that a person can manage half a kilo of weight for every year of his age – but as the writers of this book grow older, they find this formula less and less attractive! The truth is that physical strength – as well as the ability to struggle on without moaning – varies widely from individual to individual, so it is no use relying on a rule of thumb. You simply have to judge your own ability.

All that can be said with certainty is that every little bit of weight you can save will make each day's journey that much more comfortable; although for a lightweight camping holiday lasting two or three weeks, it is very doubtful whether you will be able to reduce your load to less than 9 kg (20 lb). The weights shown in the checklist set out opposite are about average and produce a total, for each of two companions travelling together, of around 11 kg (25 lb).

If during experiments you find that this is more than you can easily manage, consider going on holiday in a group of three people instead of two. Provided that the tent is big enough for three, this reduces individual loads even further. The other two people may also be able to shoulder a few extra pounds in order to lighten your share.

Limiting the carrying-distance also helps. In any case, it is always advisable to plan your holiday so that you do not have to walk or cycle very far in the first few days, to give the body some running-in time. During your practice excursions you can check what distance you cover in an average hour at your most economical pace: then if you reckon to be on the move initially for about four hours, with periodic rests, you will be able to calculate what is an easy day's journey.

Finally, there is some scope for weight-saving on food supplies provided that you are in an area where you can rely on being able to stock up with provisions at the end of the afternoon. The rule is to eat heartily in the morning and evening when you are in camp and to exist on the minimum while you are travelling.

Checklist for backpackers and cyclists

(For two persons travelling together)

Items that can be shared :

approximate weight

	kg	lb	oz
Lightweight tent (with poles, groundsheet, pegs and flysheet)	4500	10	0
Stove (with fuel and matches)	675	1	8
Canteen (consisting of nesting pans/frypans with lids that serve as plates)	560	1	4
Can opener	55		2
Collapsible polythene bucket	55		2
Torch (with batteries)	170		6
Candle	55		2
Compass and maps	225		8
First aid dressings, aspirins, sun lotion	170		6
Toothpaste	55		2
Butter container and plastic food bags	55		2
Long term food supplies (sugar, milk powder, salt, pepper, instant coffee, instant potato, packet soups, salami, cheese spread, jam etc.)	1125	2	8
Short term food supplies (bread, butter or margarine, cheese, sliced meat, fruit, frozen vegetables etc. bought as required)	2250	5	0
Flask containing drinking water	450	1	0
Camera	400		14
Total divided between two persons	5400	12	0

Items carried separately by each person :

approximate weight

	kg	lb	oz
Rucksack or panniers	1125	2	8
Sleeping bag (in stuff sac)	1575	3	8
Warm sweater and waterproof outerclothing (more often carried than worn)	900	2	0
Spare footwear (plimsolls or sandals)	350		12
Spare woollen socks (2 or 3 pairs)	225		8
Spare underwear and swimming costume	200		7
Spare shirt or blouse	110		4
Shorts (carried while trousers are worn)	225		8
Sunglasses and case	85		3
Sunhat	55		2
Small towel	110		4
Soap and toothbrush	55		2
Razor	55		2
Sleeping mat	450	1	0
Clip-together alloy knife, fork and spoon	85		3
Plastic plate	55		2
Plastic mug	55		2
Paper handkerchiefs (for use as handkerchiefs, toilet paper and for cleaning and drying utensils etc.)	55		2
Passport	55		2
Ballpoint pen	25		1
Total including shared items	11250	25	0

Clothing and footwear for the walker

The chances that while on a camping holiday you will receive an invitation to dine with the French President or attend the Hunt Ball are fortunately rather small. So all the "dressing up" clothes can be left at home and your outfit can be confined to the strictly practical. For winter holidays and mountaineering, high quality clothing is essential but for summer conditions what you wear is to a large extent a matter of personal taste.

In principle, for camping and living outdoors you just need three layers: a thin one for hot days; a thicker one for protection against cool winds and light showers; and a truly waterproof one for prolonged rain. The simplest combinations are shorts and tee-shirt; jeans, pullover and/or anorak; and a nylon cagoule plus waterproof overtrousers. It should be mentioned, however, that tight jeans are not ideal for walking in as they do not provide either enough insulation when it is cold and wet or enough ventilation when it is hot and sticky. The traditional hiking outfit consists of thicker, more generously cut trousers that buckle just below the knee, combined with long woollen socks. But it depends whether you feel chic enough in this garb or whether an Italian jump-suit is more in your line.

Still on the practical side, three changes of socks and underwear may be about all you can carry; and a spare patterned shirt that does not immediately look untidy if it is slept in or worn for several days. The socks should preferably be made from wool as nylon tends to chafe and feel hot. You also need a swimming costume; probably sunglasses and a sunhat; and then of course a stout pair of walking boots or shoes.

Footwear should be the best you can afford and the most important point is that it should be a little larger than your normal size to allow for swelling. It should also not be absolutely new and unworn at the start of a holiday. Boots should have been "broken in" first, otherwise they are liable to be uncomfortable and to cause troublesome blisters. If they are well rubbed with dubbin or wetproof silicone shoe polish before you set out and then again at regular intervals, they will not soak up moisture so easily in damp conditions.

*Left:
lightweight
walking boot.
Sewn-in tongue.
Hook lacing.
1120 g/pair*

*Left:
light canvas
desert boot.
Lace-ups.
1040 g/pair*

*Below: robust
leather boot.
Padded upper.
2250 g/pair*

*gaiters prevent
water, snow
and stones
from entering*

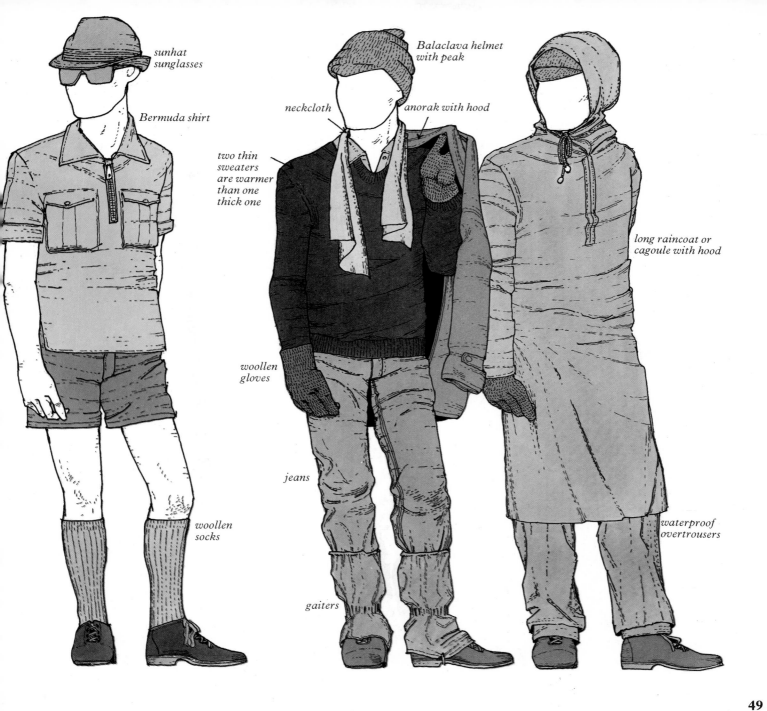

sunhat
sunglasses

Bermuda shirt

Balaclava helmet
with peak

neckcloth

anorak with hood

two thin
sweaters
are warmer
than one
thick one

woollen
gloves

long raincoat or
cagoule with hood

jeans

woollen
socks

waterproof
overtrousers

gaiters

Choosing and packing a rucksack

The rucksack in which you are going to carry all your equipment should be chosen with care. There are a great many different sizes and designs on the market, so have a good look at catalogues describing them. It is also a good idea to go along to a specialist camping shop and actually try a few to see if they fit comfortably on your back.

You will want to choose a sack which is large enough to hold all your equipment inside it, with the exception perhaps of your tent which on some models is meant to be strapped on underneath the sack. There is no point in setting off looking like a tinker's caravan, with pots and pans swinging about loose and hampering your stride. It is also helpful if the interior of the rucksack is divided up into two or three compartments so that you can find things in it more easily and quickly.

Pockets on the outside are also good for storing smaller items which you may want to get at quickly. While you are on the move, these encourage you not to stuff odd bits and pieces into your trouser pockets or sling them around your neck; and in camp they are the backpacker's equivalent of drawers and cupboards so that you always know where to lay hands on the can opener or the matches. Only climbers and potholers may need to avoid rucksacks with outside pockets, for fear that they may perhaps snag on protruding rocks.

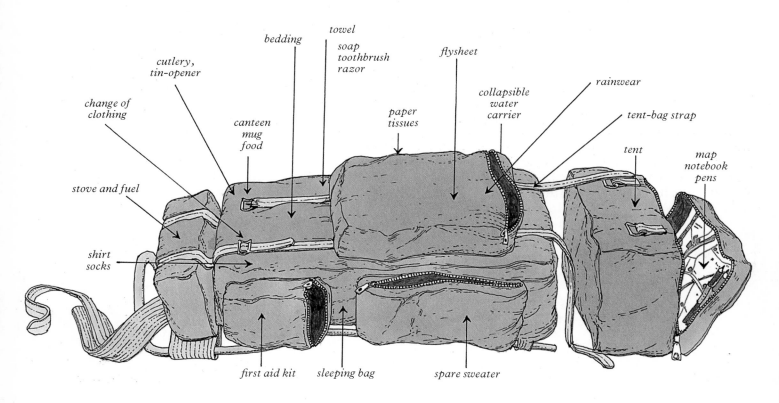

The anatomy of the backpack

The reason why backpackers are *back*-packers and not suitcase-porters is that strain is chiefly felt by the human body when its muscles have to pull against a weight that is forcing it off balance. The closer any burden is placed to the vertical line between head and feet, the less its effects will be noticeable since it will be supported by the body's bone-structure rather than the muscles. If a large portion of the weight can be rested on the hips rather than on the back or shoulders, that is even better. The spinal column is not a rigid support and requires a certain amount of muscle power to hold it up even when it is not carrying anything extra.

Again if two people are holidaying together, they may not need to choose identical rucksacks. One could be, say, of the type which has the sack fastened by clevis pins onto a tubular pack frame and on which there is a special space for the rolled-up tent. The other could be a sack with an internal frame. If one sack is rather bigger than the other, the smaller one can be used for day trips at other times of the year, or when short excursions are undertaken from a fixed camp.

The most critical factors affecting the comfort of a rucksack during use are the shape and position of the hip support; the padding and amount of adjustment available in the shoulder straps; and the provision of webbing or padding to prevent hard objects inside the sack from digging into the wearer's back.

Apart from these points, you will need to check the weight of the rucksack – it should be as light as possible without being flimsily made; the quality of the materials – usually nylon cloth and straps these days as they are both tough and waterproof; the strength of the frame and the stitching and the quality of any zip fasteners; the special reinforcement of stress points and the base of the sack; and whether the top flap is generous enough to stop water entering even when the mouth of the sack is fully extended. Although most rucksacks are indeed designed to be waterproof, the cautious backpacker will give his sleeping bag double protection by wrapping it in a polythene bag as well as its stuff sac. A soaked sleeping bag is quite unusable and may take a long time to dry out.

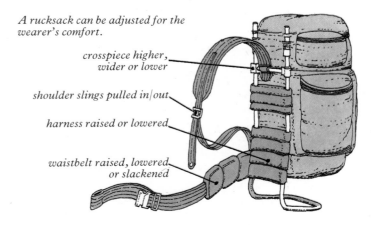

A rucksack can be adjusted for the wearer's comfort.

crosspiece higher, wider or lower

shoulder slings pulled in/out

harness raised or lowered

waistbelt raised, lowered or slackened

Left :
dayhiking rucksack with aluminium
frame (capacity 19 litres).

Below left :
large capacity interior frame
rucksack (about 65 litres).

Centre :
basic external frame (weight 1000g)
as incorporated in the rucksack shown
on the right.

Right :
large capacity sack with external pack
frame. Separate tent bag on top
(about 75 litres).

52

Two-person lightweight tents

After a comfortable rucksack, the lightweight camper's next priority is a night-time place to shelter. In fact it is possible to risk sleeping out of doors without a tent in the summer under the semi-protection of trees or a hedgerow but the odds against being able to do this for the whole of a three-week holiday, without having to endure a soaking, are fairly high. The exercise also requires each person to have a good quality sleeping bag that will not be penetrated by dew, so if shortage of money is the problem it may be more effective for two friends to share the cost of a cheap make-do tent and for them to improvise the sleeping bags.

The simplest form of lightweight tent is the two-pole ridge tent. It looks like a sheet hung over a low washing line and pegged to the ground at an angle on either side. But of course there are many other designs and adaptations produced by different manufacturers (see illustrations overleaf), including wedge shapes, bell ends, single poles, transverse ridges, domes, tunnels and kennels.

Flysheets, groundsheets and A-poles

Although a weight of 4.5 kilos was given in the equipment checklist on page 47, some specialist tents weigh as little as half or even a third of that amount. This can be achieved nowadays by making them out of polyurethane- or silicone-proofed nylon, and generally standards of manufacture are very high. But the backpacker or cyclist should think twice before buying a tent without a tough, sewn-in groundsheet. A large protective flysheet which extends right down to the ground is also worth the effort of the extra couple of pounds. As well as making the tent less transparent, warmer and more rain and windproof, a flysheet with a front or side extension provides an undercover space in which to stow your gear or shelter your cooking apparatus during any bad weather.

Below left: low priced, single skinned, two-pole ridge tent with groundsheet. Right: a similar size tent but with separate flysheet, sidewalls and front canopy.

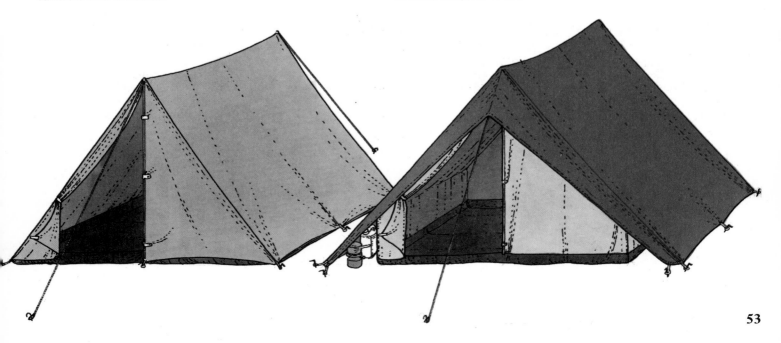

A great deal of trouble has also been taken by manufacturers to develop "Ripstop" and other lightweight nylon materials which "breathe" in the same way as the much heavier canvas that is traditionally used for frame tents. However, because the volume of air inside a low ridge tent is fairly small it can still rather easily become saturated with moisture that condenses on the cold fabric when the door is zipped up and two people are sleeping inside. In order to minimise this problem, look for a tent which has fair-sized ventilation panels made from insect-proof mesh. Also check whether the entrance zip of the inner tent closes upwards from the bottom: if it does, it can often be left partially open without the fear that rain will enter.

With some models of lightweight tent, you may be offered A-poles – or angle poles – as an alternative to the simple upright poles that support the ridge. By bridging the entrance or the interior space, although they again add an extra pound or two to the weight, A-poles give you greater freedom of movement inside, and with the single-pole type of tent they may actually make it possible to fit in an extra person.

Options such as this are much easier to take a decision on if you can actually see the tent erected and creep inside it, so it may be worth travelling some distance to a showroom or display area where this is possible. There are also camping exhibitions from time to time. Before you complete your purchase, however, do not forget the opposite consideration: i.e. look at the packed-up size of tent and poles to make sure that they will fit into your rucksack.

Also pause for a moment to think about the colour of your tent. Bright orange nylon may look very cheerful but it is also quite conspicuous, not to say an eyesore, in a green landscape. In theory, as a backpacker you should always ask the permission of the local landowner before camping wild but whether the land is publicly or privately owned you may still not want to stand out like an orchid in an onion patch.

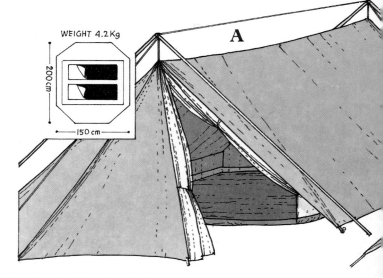

A   Double-skinned nylon ridge tent with sewn-in groundsheet with A-poles and flysheet which extends down to the ground for protection and storage.

B   Single pole tent with sewn-in groundsheet. This design is slightly less stable in high winds than a two-pole ridge tent but has more headroom in the centre and enough space for three persons if the single pole is replaced by A-poles.

C   High quality transverse ridge tent with an entrance on both sides and ample stowage space.

D   Dome tent with shock-cord linked alloy pole sections. The flysheet can be pitched first to form a large shelter before the inner tent is erected.

E   Tunnel tent with fibreglass supporting hoops and a wide valance which allows it to be weighted with rocks for greater security on hard ground and under mountainous conditions.

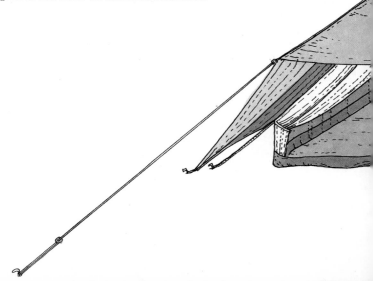

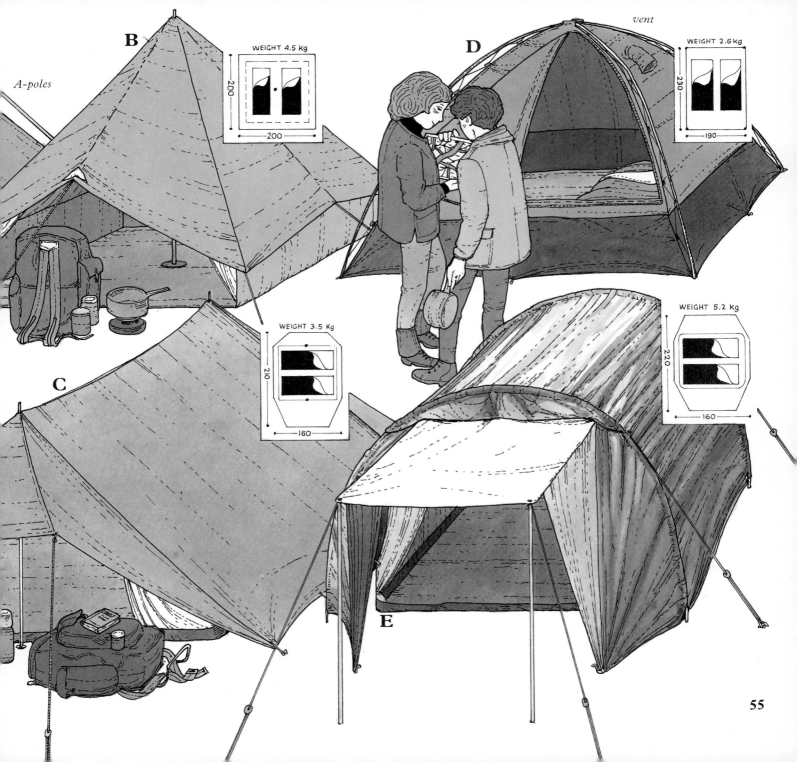

A-poles

B

WEIGHT 4.5 kg

200

200

vent

D

WEIGHT 2.6 kg

230

190

WEIGHT 3.5 Kg

210

160

C

WEIGHT 5.2 kg

220

160

E

Inside the sleeping bag

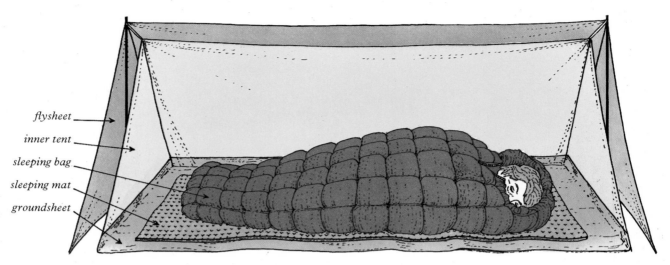

flysheet
inner tent
sleeping bag
sleeping mat
groundsheet

Having wrapped two layers of nylon tent around himself, the next thing the lightweight camper needs is a warm bed in which to rest his tired and blistered body. Just like the family camper in a frame tent, he has to insulate himself not only against the chill night air but also against the coldness of the ground. He is however handicapped by not having room on his back or pannier frame for a campbed, a mattress and a bulky quilt-type sleeping bag, so some sort of compromise has to be found.

The best that can be done in the way of a mattress is a roll-up foam mat or an inflatable button bed (see illustrations), supplemented by a thick pullover or any other piece of spare clothing that will soften the ground. Then on top of these comes a close-fitting lightweight sleeping bag that, for the sake of economy, tapers towards the foot end. Once inside such a bag, the camper looks ludicrously like an Egyptian mummy but fortunately because of its warm construction he will also be able to sleep like one.

Virtually all good bags not only consist of two layers of fabric stuffed with a highly insulating filler but are divided internally into separate cells. This prevents the filler from migrating around inside and leaving thin cold spots without any insulation at all. In some high quality bags designed for extreme conditions there are even two separate layers of cells, the middle of one cell overlapping the seam of the other so as to reduce heat loss to a minimum.

These Super Sub Zero Arctic Specials are as treasured as teddy bears by the hardened winter backpacker. They are warm and cuddly, have a hood that wraps around the head and shoulders of the sleeper and seem to weigh hardly anything. They also compress into a remarkably small stuff sac for daytime stowage but their great drawback is that, being filled with the highest grade of goose and duck down, they are disproportionately expensive.

Snuggling up without down

For a lightweight sleeping bag you must certainly expect to have to pay more than for an ordinary quilt type, but as a beginner you need not spend an absolute fortune. Most summer holidays do not require something of polar quality nor is it worthwhile to double your expenditure for the sake of a marginal saving in weight. Down-filled bags are still regarded as the best but not by such a large margin as a few years ago. Some excellent man-made fibre fillers have been developed with similar properties to natural down. Typical are the "Hollofil" tubular fibres which have the ability to expand again after they have been compressed many times and to trap pockets of air, which is the real secret of insulation.

You should consult a specialist camping shop about these latest developments in case a better-quality man-made filling is preferable to a poorer-quality down filling. At present man-made sacks weigh more and do not squeeze into the small space of a down sack. However, they are more easily washed and are less disastrously affected if they get wet. Man-made fibres are in any case the only choice for certain people who find that they are allergic to down, and some fibres may recommend themselves through being easier to clean.

When you visit a large shop you will have the advantage of seeing a whole row of different sleeping bags hung up on a rail. This is the way they should be stored at home so that their filling is not squashed for months on end but in the shop it is done to help you compare lengths and sizes. If you are tall, choosing a bag that you fit into is more important than having the warmest possible filling. The filling can be of the highest specifications but it will still not prevent you from shivering if your shoulders poke out of the top.

A mummy-style bag with an integral hood needs to have an overall length 30 cm (1 ft) greater than your height. A narrow, pointed bag should have a tailored toe piece to accommodate your feet; by selecting a wider bag, even if it s not so heavily insulated, you will also have room to wear extra clothes inside it on exceptionally cold nights.

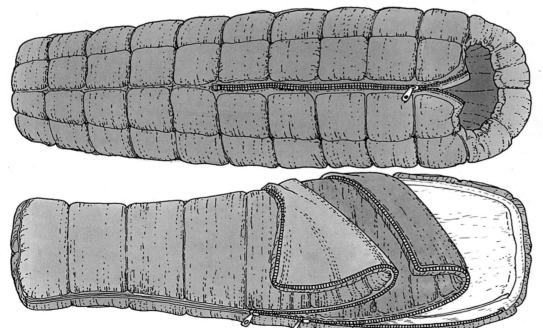

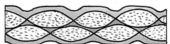

Left and above: mummy-style bag and its cellular structure. Weight 1800g.

Above: lightweight foam mattress. Weight 320g.

Left: two sleeping bags in one; two sets of four layers each. One set can be removed in warmer weather and used as a mattress. Weight 2300g.

Stoves and utensils

In some locations, lighting a campfire is not a sin and if it can be done without any danger of burning down a forest or leaving an unsightly area of singed grass and blackened stones, every lightweight camper should try it some time. It makes for a perfect ending to an outdoor day. Moreover the fuel is free and can be picked up off the ground in the form of fallen twigs and pinecones: it does not have to be carried all the way from home.

If you intend to have a campfire, pack a folded sheet of cooking foil among your utensils. It can be used to wrap potatoes, fish and other items of food which are then placed in the glowing embers to roast. Backpacker-sized pans can be heated directly over a very small fire or they can be balanced on stones at the edge of a larger fire and have hot embers raked under them. In the meantime, while the coffee is brewing, you can be cooking sausages by toasting them on the end of a sharpened stick.

For more everyday cooking you need a lightweight stove and a portable supply of fuel. There is a choice of ones that burn petrol (gas in America), paraffin (kerosene) and methylated spirit – which are all volatile liquid fuels that should be handled responsibly. The liquids can easily contaminate foods, so the stove with attached tank, plus any flask containing extra fuel, should be kept in a separate compartment of either rucksack or panniers.

Any pouring should be done well away from naked flames, and particularly in the case of a petrol stove you should study the operating instructions carefully. It is possible to cause a shooting flame on some models by overfilling the fuel tank and so allowing non-vapourised fuel to get through to the burner. Another danger may arise from using ordinary gas-station petrol, which motorcyclists may be tempted to do since they have a constant supply available: not only lead but other additives cause unhealthy fumes so it is advisable to buy special additive-free petrol or at least give the stove lots of air when cooking.

Of the other types of stove, one of the cheapest – although it heats rather slowly – is the methylated spirit picnic stove. Cheaper still is the one you can make yourself out of an old tin can which burns "meta" solid fuel. Bars or tablets of this can be bought in packs and a 50-bar pack weighs only 225 g (8 oz). However, each of these types is really only adequate for fair-weather cooking, when waiting times are not critical, although a miniature meta-burning stove can be an emergency standby. For greater convenience, liquefied butane gas again scores over other kinds of fuel, just as it did for frame tent campers. The Globetrotter stove by Camping Gaz International weighs only 450 g (1 lb) and burns continuously for up to 1 hr 40 mins using the miniature GT cartridge – not perhaps quite as long when it is turned up to full heat but quite adequate if you are prepared to keep another cartridge in reserve.

Cooking in half a nutshell
The Globetrotter stove is actually sold together with a pair of miniature pans which it neatly packs into for carriage. But for increasing its capacity and for cooking on other stoves you will need to purchase a separate set of pans. Families travelling by car have room to take along ordinary utensils from the home kitchen but backpackers and cyclists will find these too cumbersome. It is better to invest in a canteen of aluminium pans, frypans and lids which are specially designed to nest into each other and save space as well as weight.

For two people it is advisable to have at least two saucepans (one for boiling water and one for cooking food) and two matching lids which can also act as either frypans or deep plates. The lids are essential and should always be kept in place, otherwise you will

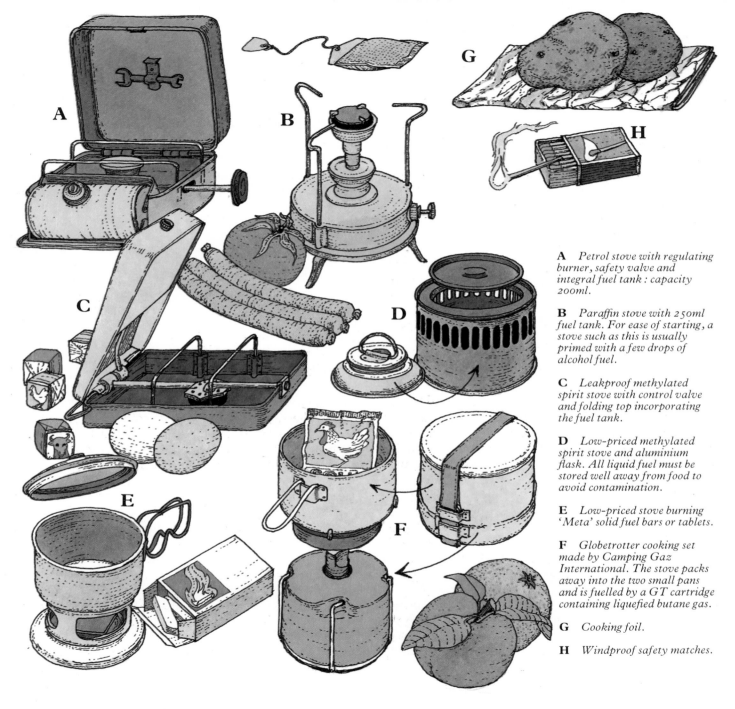

A Petrol stove with regulating burner, safety valve and integral fuel tank: capacity 200ml.

B Paraffin stove with 250ml fuel tank. For ease of starting, a stove such as this is usually primed with a few drops of alcohol fuel.

C Leakproof methylated spirit stove with control valve and folding top incorporating the fuel tank.

D Low-priced methylated spirit stove and aluminium flask. All liquid fuel must be stored well away from food to avoid contamination.

E Low-priced stove burning 'Meta' solid fuel bars or tablets.

F Globetrotter cooking set made by Camping Gaz International. The stove packs away into the two small pans and is fuelled by a GT cartridge containing liquefied butane gas.

G Cooking foil.

H Windproof safety matches.

59

waste fuel through heat loss when cooking in the open and the food will cool rapidly when removed from the burner. Handles should of course not stick out when the canteen is packed together, so they need to be either hinged or detachable.

In addition, for stirring and chopping the food and for eating it when it is ready you should have at least one knife, fork and spoon each. Ordinary stainless steel cutlery is fairly serviceable but you can reduce the weight fractionally with a clip-together camping cutlery set. A separate sharp, serrated kitchen knife is also useful as you are likely to do a lot of bread, salami and fruit slicing during your holiday – in fact, a pocket knife with a built-in can opener, corkscrew and bottle opener may be a convenient multi-purpose tool.

Unless it is safe to build a campfire, the amount of cooking that can be done by lightweight campers is restricted by the quantity of fuel that can be carried. When you are on the move and out of reach of shops, hot meals can be summed up in half a nutshell: packet soups, instant mash and streaky bacon – though there are, of course, other special dehydrated foods. In fixed camps closer to civilisation the scope is much wider. You still have to keep to dishes that have short

cooking times but their packaged weight ceases to be a problem. The larder can be stocked up with cans of baked beans, stew etc. and partly-cooked frozen foods can be ferried in from the local village store. For breakfast there can be sizzling sausages, scrambled eggs and fried tomatoes – which may make it worthwhile to invest in non-stick utensils which are easier to clean.

After breakfast each morning, make a practice of collecting together empty cans, cartons and bottles and taking them with you for disposal in a litter bin. If this is not possible because your route is through open country, take the trouble to bury the litter deep in the ground. One of the cans can be used as a digging implement.

The night is another country

It was mentioned earlier on that canoe campers could enjoy a new view of a familiar landscape by seeing it from the angle of the water, and a similar experience is available to backpackers and cyclists too. Even if they are camping not far from home, all they have to do for a change is to sleep during the day and to walk or cycle during the night.

It is preferable, of course, to choose a mild moonlit night for this excursion, when a torch does not have to be used all the time and you can see well enough to avoid losing the path. But with or without the moon, the night is like a different country, full of sounds such

as those of the owl and the fox and with a perfect dramatic rhythm that seems designed to stir the human soul. It causes you to sink into shivering gloom during the early hours and then fills you full of hope again as the sky starts to lighten and the bird chorus begins.

If you can plan to be on the top of a hill just as the sun comes up, you will realise that outdoor holidays, and particularly lightweight camping, are not just about practicalities such as packing and tent-pitching: they give you access to nature and remind you that you yourself are part of the natural world.

By caravan and motor caravan

The caravan: plus and minus

Just as there are special pleasures attached to camping in a tent, holidaying in a caravan or motor caravan can be very attractive too. As children, we all loved to play in a wendy house – taking pretend tea and putting ourselves to bed in a miniature, make-believe version of our full-sized home – and this same childhood play-instinct is probably what underlies the pleasure we also obtain as adults from living in a "wendy house on wheels".

Of course, not all caravans can be described as miniature. One type is not really a mobile "van" at all, because thousands of people either own or rent *fixed* caravans which always remain on the same site, close to the sea or to some other leisure amenity. These are more like small cottages, with their own piece of garden and services such as a power supply laid on. They scarcely need a recommendation under the heading of outdoor holidays except that, like all holiday cottages, they can serve as a base from which to go sailing, swimming, riding or exploring.

The solid advantages

The truly mobile vans that holidaymakers tow behind their cars are usually referred to as touring caravans, and the name highlights one of their chief advantages over an ordinary frame tent. For people who enjoy touring – which perhaps means moving from one stopping-place to another almost every day – taking along a form of accommodation with solid, ready-erected walls does away with the constant chore of having to put up and take down a cumbersome tent. In fact, not only is a caravan ready to move into as soon as you arrive at a new site, it is also a portable restaurant-cum-motel in which to take a meal and a siesta half way through a day's journey.

Importantly, a caravan does for camping what a greenhouse does for gardening: it extends the summer by giving you better protection against the weather and allowing you to go on holiday either early or late in the season, at a time when staying in a tent might be rather damp and chilly. Many older people also feel that it gives them an Indian summer: their bones might begin to creak a little if they crept around in a tent but they are comfortably off in a caravan which raises them above ground level and allows them to sleep, sit and dine without any strain or contortions.

weeks of the year. The design of a caravan is often very pleasing in itself but its line and colouring are concepts of the coach-building and motor industry, not of architects or conservationists, so it can look as ghastly as a corrugated iron shed to your neighbours.

On the road, too, a caravan is something of a drawback to your progress. Nowadays standards of design are so high that all vans can theoretically be towed at high speed with very little danger. Nevertheless, even with a well-matched car and van you cannot legally travel at above 50 mph (about 80 kph) in some countries, including Britain, and in general the weight of a van will always cut your acceleration and in some instances reduce your speed to a crawl on steep hills.

On board ferries, caravans usually cost extra not only because they take up extra space lengthwise but because their height often makes it necessary to stow them among the heavy goods vehicles. Even more expensively nowadays, a caravan increases your fuel consumption on account of both its weight and drag-effect. Overall it can raise your petrol bill by up to a third in the case of a tall van with flat surfaces and square corners at the front and back – although many manufacturers are now actively trying to do something to reduce drag-effects.

The heavy drawbacks

Against these advantages have to be set a number of minus points about caravans. First, they are very expensive to buy: if you bought a new caravan at today's prices and rate of inflation, you would probably have to own it for about five years before you broke even with the cost of spending your summer holidays in a hotel or guesthouse. Secondly, you would need an unobtrusive place to store the van: most models are too tall and wide to fit into a domestic garage and it is not very satisfactory to have one stuck on the front lawn, blocking your windows for 45

Trailer tents and folding caravans

If your enthusiasm for owning a caravan is dampened by some or all of the above-mentioned disadvantages, you may be attracted by one of the four alternative forms of towable accommodation which reduce the problems of expense, storage and high fuel consumption. Each of them allows the older holiday-maker to live more sedately out of contact with the ground while at the same time being ready for occupation almost as quickly as a conventional caravan.

The five-minute Bedouin

A trailer tent has walls and roof made of canvas and nylon, so in this respect it is more like a standard frame tent. The difference is that it can be unfolded from its trailer in a matter of minutes and that in some models there is a wooden floor just like a caravan's. The beds are usually on platforms hinged to the top rim of the trailer and when they are folded out they are supported above the ground by adjustable steel legs.

Often the manufacturers of trailer tents offer a detachable awning which provides additional living and sleeping space. But when the tent is pitched without this – during a quick daytime or overnight stop – the ground underneath does not need to be completely level and free from bumps. Typically the height of the trailer when it is closed up for towing is only about a metre (3 ft 3 in) and it will not weigh more than 500 kg (10 cwt) including a reasonable amount of extra luggage. Both these factors make it very easy and economical to tow.

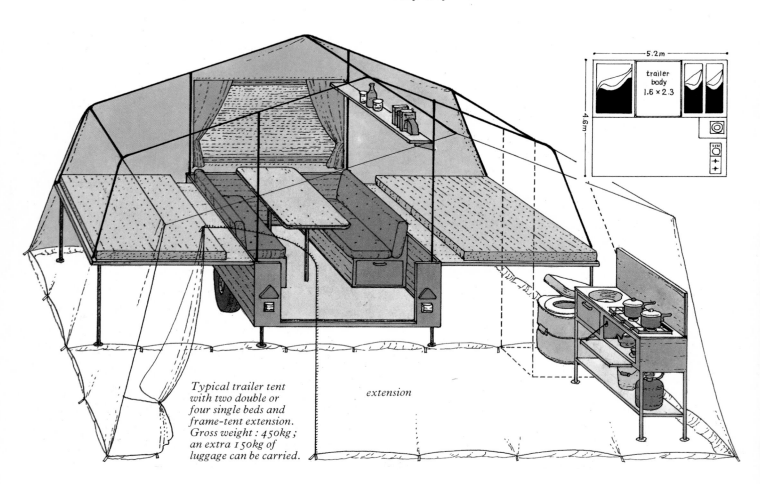

Typical trailer tent with two double or four single beds and frame-tent extension. Gross weight: 450 kg; an extra 150 kg of luggage can be carried.

extension

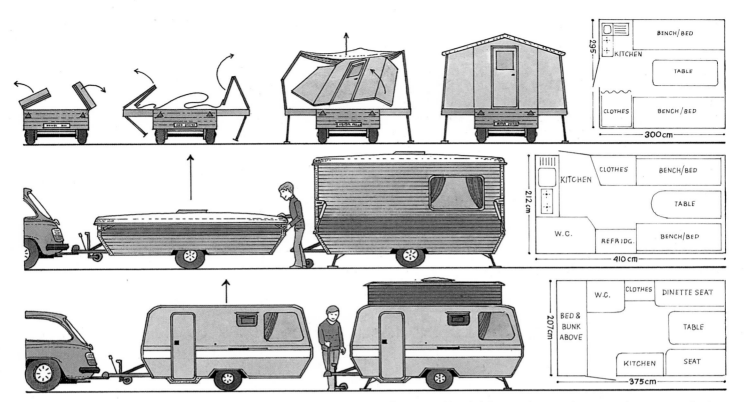

The halfway house

Two forms of folding caravan represent a genuine halfway house between the frame tent and the fully rigid caravan. The first is a solid-walled version of the trailer tent, working on exactly the same principle of having beds on platforms hinged to the rim of the trailer. Since the walls in this case have a layer of hard material on the outside as well as a certain thickness of insulation, the set-up *feels* more like a caravan, though it *looks* almost like a small chalet when a special skirt is attached to hide the trailer's undercarriage.

The second type of folding van is based on a broader and longer trailer with the same floor area as a conventional small caravan. The trick is that it is only half the height of a normal van until the roof is raised by four powerful gas struts on the corners. Then the four walls fold up into place and some of the collapsible cupboards are raised above waist height, so it is almost indistinguishable from a rigid caravan.

The low-roofed compact

Last of the four problem-solving alternatives is the recently-introduced compact caravan that simply has an elevating roof on top of a squat body. It does not pack down as low as half height like the previous type of folding van but the concertina roof means that for towing and storage its streamlined top is only 1938 mm (6 ft 4½ in) above the ground – low enough to make a considerable difference to its wind-resistance and reduce the effect on the tow-car's fuel consumption: also low enough for it to be stored in the double garage alongside your car.

Compromising with a camper

A more fundamental alternative to the caravan-and-car combination is the motor caravan. If you go on holiday in one of these, you do not need to tow any kind of trailer so, depending on the size of the vehicle and its engine power, there are fewer difficulties over storage, ferry charges and speed restrictions.

Motor caravans are usually standard commercial vehicles that have been converted for cooking, eating and sleeping in by specialist firms such as Danbury, Dormobile and CI Autohomes. The largest models, normally called motorhomes, are the size of a furniture carrier – over 3 m (10 ft) high and 10 m (33 ft) long. The smallest ones, called campers, are conversions of delivery vans and are no longer or wider than a family saloon. Like the compact caravan, they usually have an elevating roof that is left down during travel and storage and then raised to provide adequate headroom, and in some cases extra sleeping space, when the van is being used for camping.

Most people who buy a motor caravan have to compromise between their holiday camping requirements and their everyday transport needs during the rest of the year. If you are deciding which of these should have priority, everyday transport will seem at first to be more important, bearing in mind that a summer holiday lasts only three or four weeks compared with about 48 weeks of ordinary commuting, but this is an over-simplified picture. In practice on a touring holiday you may clock up about a third of your annual mileage and if you were to make use of the camper for other short breaks – an Easter trip to the coast or a long weekend in the country – the proportions would begin to work out at almost equal. On the basis of time rather than mileage, you are likely to find that you use the vehicle just as much for camping as for driving to the office, since you occupy it for virtually 24 hours a day while on holiday compared with only about one hour on a normal working day.

The result of these considerations is a true compromise and for the majority of families who want to own a motor caravan it means choosing a medium-sized camper based on a vehicle such as the Volkswagen Transporter Kombi or the Bedford CF van. It is generally possible to house these in a domestic garage and their fuel consumption is not too much higher than that of an ordinary car. They are of course cramped inside compared with a towed caravan but conversions like the CI Kamper provide quite comfortable sleeping space for two adults and two growing children. An awning can also be added to extend the van's basic living area.

One and two-piece motorhomes

Larger motorhomes are perhaps more suitable for families that can afford to keep a second car for everyday purposes. They are not ideal vehicles for driving in crowded traffic, popping round to the shops or squeezing into the office car park – in fact they do not fit into multi-storey car parks because of their height. Finally, there is yet another alternative for a couple without children: the demountable motorhome (see opposite page) which leaves its pick-up truck free to drive around independently when it is not riding piggy-back.

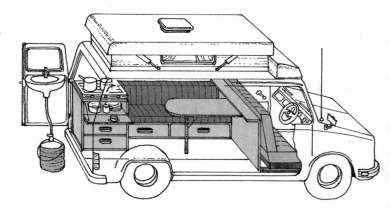

Many popular campers are based on the Volkswagen Kombi Transporter which has a side opening door. This model by CI Autohomes has a tall concertina roof which provides both good headroom and the space for an upper double bed. The interior has a built-in gas cooker and both forward and rear-facing seats which convert into the main bed.

Left and below: one of the smallest types of camper has an elevating roof so that there is enough headroom for the occupants.

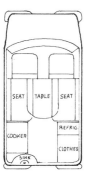

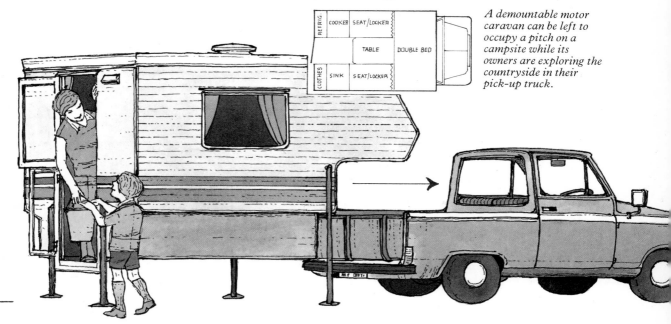

A demountable motor caravan can be left to occupy a pitch on a campsite while its owners are exploring the countryside in their pick-up truck.

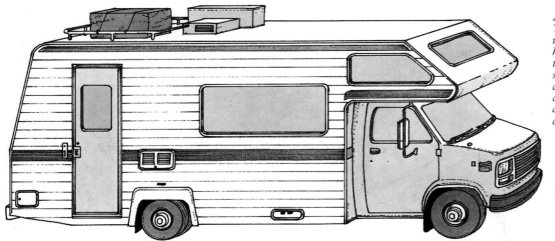

A luxury motorhome such as this Travel Cruiser is ideal for touring in the U.S.A. and Canada. It has a separate bathroom and toilet, beds for six people and a superbly equipped kitchen. One advantage over a similar-sized caravan is that safety regulations allow passengers to ride inside it during the journey.

240

686 cm

storage lockers & hi-fi unit

double bed over cab

storage

bath/shower

below : seating/double bed

cab

cooker oven

W.C.

kitchen unit

fridge/freezer space

food store

storage gas etc.

wardrobe

air conditioning/ventilation

To own a caravan or motorhome is the dream of many people who have already spent several holidays under canvas and know that they will never go back to staying at hotels. As mentioned before, it is a comfortable way for older people to go on enjoying outdoor holidays after living in a tent has become a slight hardship; but how do they, or any other potential caravan owners, find out whether caravanning really suits them? What about the legendary horrors of reversing with a caravan hitched to the car? Will they be happy enough in a small van or should they invest in something larger?

The best way to discover the answers to such questions is to hire a van for the first trial holiday. Many companies these days offer a range of ready-equipped caravans for hire, so the process of choosing and holidaying in one provides a very good rehearsal for the "real thing" without costing such a huge sum if a mistake is made. You can hire a van for a week in the spring and then buy one in time for the summer holidays: or by hiring one during the summer period you may then be in a position to pick up a bargain during the winter. A lot of good secondhand caravans come onto the market after the season is over and later in the year dealers are also more inclined to offer discounts on new vans.

What size of caravan?

Whether you need to hire a two, four or six-berth caravan should be fairly obvious from the size of your family, though when buying a van afterwards you may like to have a spare bed or slightly more space for when the children grow bigger. Hire firms do not usually go in for the very largest and most heavily equipped type of van but if you are offered a very heavy van with two pairs of wheels instead of the usual single pair, do check that it is not too difficult to manoeuvre. Most smaller and lighter vans can be manhandled into a restricted space when they are not hitched to the car. However, when there are two wheels on either side, in what is called a close-coupled arrangement, they are very stable for towing but tend to scrub the ground and require a lot of effort when you want them to execute a sharp turn.

In any case the weight of caravan that your particular car can tow is limited by its own weight and pulling power. From a legal point of view, the maximum gross weight of the van – i.e. the highest weight to which the manufacturers or the law say it may be loaded – should not exceed the kerbside – i.e. unladen – weight of the tow car. In Britain if this limit is exceeded then your road speed is not allowed to be above 40 mph (64 kph); but if the regulation is conformed with, then the speed limit is 50 mph (80 kph) provided that a '50' plate is displayed on the van's rear. The respective kerbside and maximum gross weight must also be displayed on the near-side of the car/caravan.

In practice it is advisable to stay well within the regulation and to make very careful checks if the van's actual all-up laden weight goes above three-quarters of the car's weight. It is always wise to find out what the makers of your car say that it can tow although they are concerned with mechanical ill effects on their vehicle rather than matters of stability. Their figures are therefore sometimes extremely confusing to the newcomer. You should also listen to the experienced view of the hire company's salesman unless you suspect that he is trying to "sell" you a higher category van than you actually need.

The careful matching of your car and van is important so that the combination will be stable when you are moving at speed. The weight also makes a big difference when you are starting off, climbing a hill or accelerating to overtake a slow-moving lorry. Strictly speaking, it is the engine's torque output that matters here rather than its cubic capacity, and whether the car is manual or automatic or has front wheel drive only makes a difference in exceptional circumstances. Automatic cars generally make good towers, although the automatic transmission may sometimes require additional cooling.

Recent caravans are often wedge-shaped, which reduces drag-effect and considerably improves petrol consumption.

Sometimes the same basic model is available with alternative interior layouts. The caravan shown opposite provides luxury accommodation for 2 people in an internal space measuring 192 cm high, 428 cm long and 195 cm wide. The alternative version (see drawing below) accommodates up to 5 people in the same area.

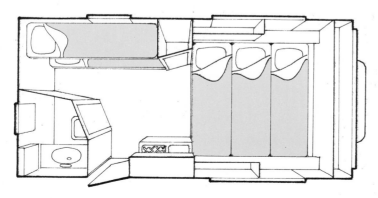

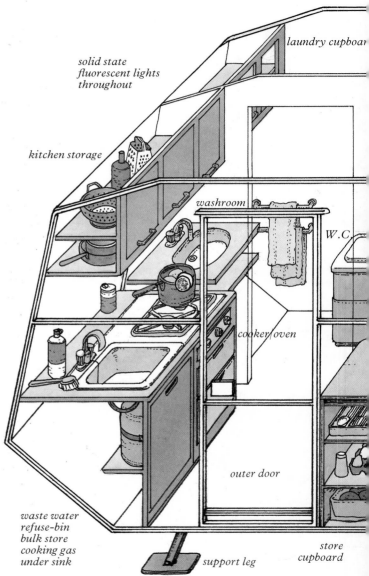

solid state fluorescent lights throughout

laundry cupboard

kitchen storage

washroom

W.C

cooker/oven

outer door

waste water
refuse-bin
bulk store
cooking gas
under sink

support leg

store cupboard

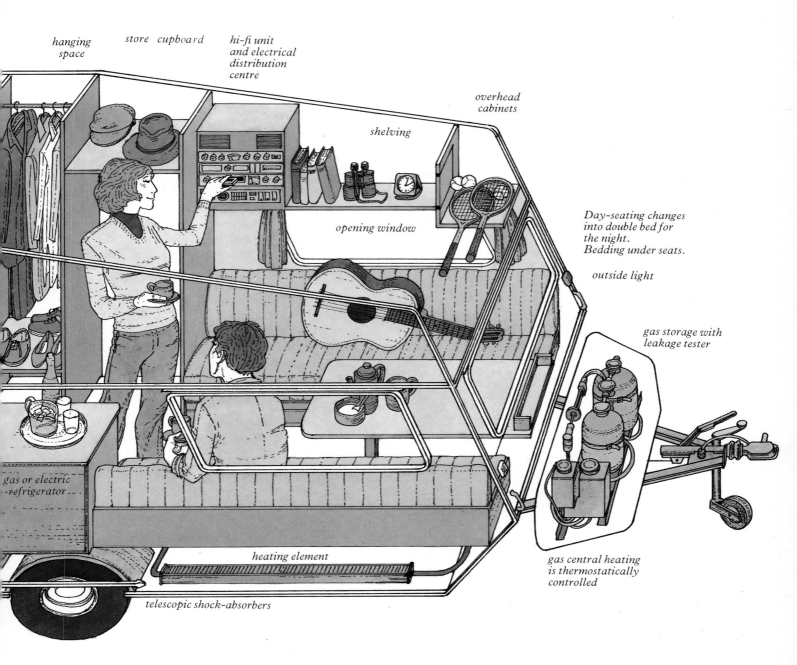

hanging space

store cupboard

hi-fi unit and electrical distribution centre

overhead cabinets

shelving

Day-seating changes into double bed for the night. Bedding under seats.

outside light

gas storage with leakage tester

opening window

gas or electric refrigerator

heating element

gas central heating is thermostatically controlled

telescopic shock-absorbers

Features and fittings

Virtually all modern caravans have upholstered benches at one end underneath a broad picture window so that the occupants can sit there in luxury in the "dinette" and enjoy the surrounding scenery. This attractive feature is probably the first one that everybody looks for when selecting a van but there are a number of practical considerations too.

Cooler driving, warmer living

Two factors that affect driving are the aerodynamic shape of the van and how difficult it is to see through from front to back. With fuel bills in mind, look at whether the manufacturers have reduced the drag-effect by rounding the corners or inclining the roof at the front to allow air to stream over the top; are the fore and aft windows set low enough to allow you to see right through the van when you glance in the rear view mirror? If not, you will need to fit extending wing mirrors or a periscope mirror to your car and there will still be inevitable blindspots.

In the general construction of the caravan not all the workmanship will be visible so you may need to read through the manufacturer's specifications to see how much attention has been paid to rustproofing and insulation. A few vans have double glazing and are specially designed for comfort even in winter; if you wish to go caravanning all the year round, you may think their high cost worthwhile.

At least it must be assumed that you will want to go touring in the spring and autumn when roads and campsites are less crowded. You may be a sporting enthusiast who can use his caravan at various times of the year for attending golf tournaments, rallycross meetings and showjumping events. For these purposes you need a reasonable degree of insulation in the floor, walls and roof, and this also helps to keep the van cooler in summer if it is accompanied by proper ventilation.

Look at the area of openable windows, the size of the roof light and whether the top half of the door can be opened separately. Are there any openings fitted with mosquito-proof mesh for use at night? And is there a built-in heater or a place where one can be attached?

A few high quality caravans have central heating which runs off a gas burner in a separate vented compartment: otherwise unvented burners inside the van can be dangerous because they consume oxygen and give off carbon monoxide. A burnerless type called a catalytic heater is usually recommended for daytime use and a "Trumatic" type heater, with external combustion and exhaust, is suitable for all-night heating.

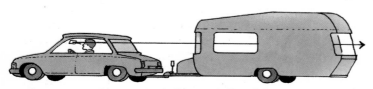

Above: car and caravan windows are aligned for good rearward vision. Below: if caravan windows are higher, a special rear view mirror is required.

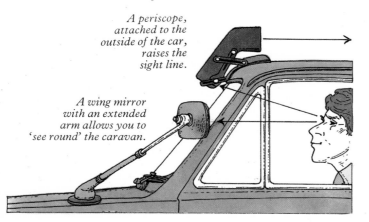

A periscope, attached to the outside of the car, raises the sight line.

A wing mirror with an extended arm allows you to 'see round' the caravan.

heater

leakage tester

The caravan kitchen

The gas supply for the majority of caravans comes from a large pressurised cylinder that is housed in a box on top of the tow bar. This is a sensible place for it because it reduces the chance of leaks inside the van and makes it easy to carry out replacement of an empty cylinder in the open air out of reach of naked flames. The gas is piped through to the kitchen area where there is a two-burner hob and a small refrigerator (very desirable during hot summers) that also runs off the butane supply. The majority of caravans do not have an oven as this would take up valuable space and consume rather a lot of gas, but an oven can be fitted should you require one. For many caravanners it is more important to ensure that there is a grill for making toast etc.: vans made on the European continent tend to lack this facility.

The kitchen area is very compact and is usually positioned in the middle of a side wall of the caravan, close to the door. This too is a practical location since it is over the axle where the balance of the van will not be disturbed when a load of shopping is packed on board. If you choose a caravan that has the kitchen located at one end, you may have to give a little more thought to day-to-day variations in loading.

To one side of the hob there may be a small folding table-top, which is very useful for the preparation of food: there should also be a splashboard to protect the wall and a window that opens to let out steam. To the other side of the cooker will be a small sink and drainer, the sink having a collapsible curved water spout that is operated by a foot pump or, more probably, an electric pump.

The water supply in a caravan is limited by the capacity of the plastic container which is either placed outside the van or kept under the sink. First-time caravanners will begin by using up the container at a rapid rate – until they discover that fresh water has to be lugged for half a mile. Thereafter, consumption will drop miraculously. Another encouragement to economy is that dirty water from the sink (and the handbasin and shower) runs out into a bucket or rubberised bottle that is placed underneath the van, and this too has to be carried away and emptied down an appropriate drain.

The lucky inhabitants of Norway, Sweden and Finland have so many clean lakes that they can bathe in and so many trees that they can disappear behind that it is surprising that bathroom fittings are sold at all in their countries. The writers of this book firmly believe this is the reason why northerners invented the sauna – so that their marketing men would have some form of hygien to sell that did not just exist naturally by the wayside!

Showers and toilets

Caravanners are like Scandinavians in this respect: they have the great outdoors for their ablutions if they are camping wild (with the landowner's permission, of course); and they have excellent toilet facilities within easy reach if they are staying at any half-decent campsite. Nevertheless, manufacturers do find it profitable to market caravans with shower and toilet compartments: people seem to want them despite the precious space they take up.

If you fear that you may be caught in a treeless landscape or that it is bound to rain when you are on your way to the service block, then a toilet compartment is seriously worth having. It should be equipped with one of the modern chemical toilets which are safe and hygienic to use. These sterilise and dissolve the waste into an inoffensive liquid which then has to be poured, as soon as the reservoir is full, either into the special disposal outlet on a campsite or into an ordinary flush toilet that is connected to the sewage system. It must not be dumped into a stream since the unspent chemicals would be harmful, or into a toilet which runs into a septic tank, because there the chemicals would interfere with the tank's bacteriological action.

For saving space but still having your own sanitation, the alternative is to hire or buy a separate toilet tent that can be pitched next to your caravan. It provides greater privacy if visitors are entertained in the van; owners of trailer tents may favour this solution too as they do not have a built-in compartment. There will be room to transport it in the trailer together with the chemical toilet.

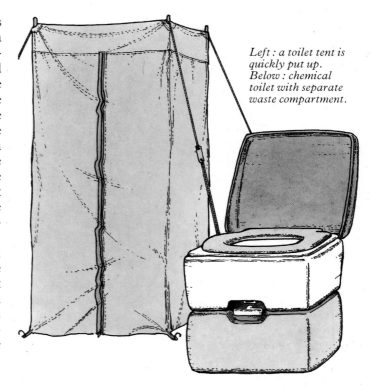

Left : a toilet tent is quickly put up. Below : chemical toilet with separate waste compartment.

The caravan after dark

With or without its own toilet, a caravan is quite like a house in that it stays warm for a while after the sun has gone down. Caravanners therefore tend to remain up, talking and reading after dark for much longer than their friends who are camping in tents. When choosing a van, you should check whether it has a lighting system and power supply that will enable you to do this.

Lighting and power supplies
Most caravans are equipped with two or three fluorescent light fittings as standard since these are the most efficient type. They consume fairly little current in relation to their light output and if they are fixed high up near the ceiling they give good overall illumination. A gas lantern may be provided as a standby or in some economy caravans the lighting may be entirely by gas, so you may want to buy an extra lantern for creating a pleasant atmosphere when you are relaxing after a meal in the dinette. It is also not difficult to fit a fluorescent light yourself.

Power for the lights and electric water pump can come via a connecting cable from your 12-volt car battery. More often there is a separate car-type battery in the caravan so that you do not run the risk of not being able to start the car in the morning. In this case, the second battery has to be charged up somehow – by a battery charger before you set off from home or by drawing current from the car's alternator as you drive along. This last method, though, is not just a matter of running in an extra wire from the car. There has to be a means of preventing electricity from being drawn back into the car's circuits from the caravan battery or vice versa. This may be a device incorporating a blocking diode or it may be a voltage-controlled relay in the circuit from the car alternator.

On the European mainland it is quite common for campsites to have sockets where caravans can be plugged in to the mains, so if you select a caravan made in a Continental country it may be equipped with a suitable connection and cable enabling you to fit a charger control box to the caravan and to recharge the battery on site.

Sleeping arrangements

When parents expect to sit up after their children have gone to bed, the youngsters' beds should be separate from the dinette area. Almost invariably it is the dinette that converts into the caravan's main double bed, usually when the table is lowered to the same height as the benches and the seat backrests are spread over it to form a continuous mattress. If the children's beds are canvas "stretchers", designed to be attached high up in the same area, then everybody has to go to bed at the same time. But in most four-berth caravans there is a separate pair of bench seats which convert into single beds; and they may have backrests supported by wooden sections that lift up and convert into pullman bunks.

Not a great deal of privacy can be attained in any caravan arrangement but a few models do have a pull-out screen that turns the dinette into a closed-off, though not soundproof, sleeping compartment. A carpeted interior also deadens the sound a little and makes the van feel luxurious, but many experienced caravanners prefer removable slip mats and vinyl flooring which are easier to keep clean.

Vinyl and other plastics are used a great deal in caravan fittings, and smokers should note that nearly all caravan mattresses are made of plastic foam. Even the upholstery may not be as fire-resistant as it should be, so smoking needs to be done with care in the confined space. If you are hiring a van, you should perhaps make sure that there is a handy fire blanket or extinguisher; and when buying, you should first of all look for a safety-conscious manufacturer and then attach extra ashtrays in strategic places. If a fire does start, there is no room for heroics and everyone must be got out immediately.

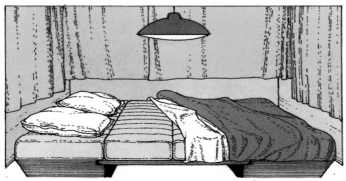

Preparing for the road

Safety aspects to do with roadworthiness are well taken care of in the modern caravan. When you hire a van, you should notify the company with whom you insure your car but they will not normally require an additional premium. The insurance for the caravan will be part of the hire charge so you need only discuss with the hire firm what exactly is covered.

Your main contribution to safety – and unavoidable expense – will be to have a properly designed towing bracket fixed to your car. On no account should you try to construct the bar yourself. Towing brackets are designed in close liaison with car manufacturers, who know exactly what stresses their vehicles can accept – and where. The *fitting* of the bracket is a job you can carry out yourself but this too is probably best left to an experienced mechanic who has the right tools and can usually complete the work in less than two hours.

If the cost is irksome, bear in mind that it is a once-and-for-all expense and that in order to save money you can spare yourself the cost of special bedding for your caravan holiday. A family hiring a frame tent for the first time has to buy a complete set of sleeping bags whereas you can, at a pinch, take along ordinary sheets, quilts and blankets.

How the tow bar works
The projecting bracket that has been attached to your car is actually the simpler half of the coupling arrangement that enables you to tow the caravan

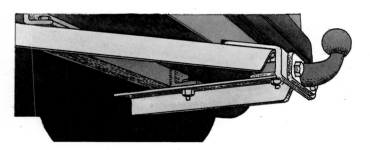

safely. It carries just two "working parts": a ball-shaped protrusion 50 mm (2 in) in diameter and a covered seven-pin electric socket that is wired up to your car's indicators and rear lights. There may also be a second seven-pin socket for supplying services in the caravan.

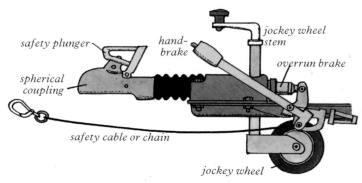

safety plunger
hand-brake
jockey wheel stem
overrun brake
spherical coupling
safety cable or chain
jockey wheel

Extending from the front of the caravan is the other half of the arrangement: a cable (or cables) with a matching plug which fastens into the seven-pin socket; and a tow bar with an inverted cup at its tip that slips over the 50 mm (2 in) ball and locks into place to form a secure, flexible joint. The tow bar also carries a jockey-wheel that can be raised and lowered by turning a handle: when the wheel is down it supports the front end of the van which is slightly nose-heavy; when it is wound up, it allows the job of supporting the caravan's front end to be gently taken over by the tow car.

Projecting from the top of the tow bar there is also a long handbrake lever: this must be applied to hold the van in position whenever it is not hitched to the car. The final and most important item incorporated in the bar is the overrun brake mechanism. This is a spring plunger covered by a concertina-shaped sleeve which applies the brakes on the caravan's wheels whenever the van presses towards the rear of the car (i.e. whenever the car slows down, the van tends to catch up with it slightly and its brakes are automatically applied). The result is that in spite of the extra weight, the braking system of the car-and-caravan combination is almost as safe and efficient as that of the car by itself.

A locking device on the ball coupling makes it impossible, under normal circumstances, for the caravan to break free from the tow car accidentally but just in case it should do so, there is a safety chain that can be attached to the towing bracket. This chain is not intended to be strong enough to pull the van. In an emergency its links will part, but before they do so the tension on the chain will have applied the caravan's brakes to prevent it from careering off the road or into the path of other traffic.

Balancing and hitching up the van

The process of hitching the van to the car is shown in the accompanying illustrations. On firm ground it can usually be managed by one person, but it should always be preceded by a check of the van's noseweight which affects the smoothness of the towing. The manufacturers will have specified the best noseweight for your particular caravan and it is important to adjust the balance of goods stowed on board until you are very near to this and certainly never short of it.

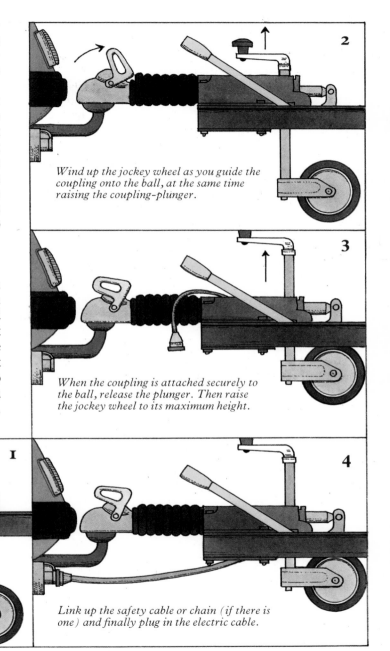

2

Wind up the jockey wheel as you guide the coupling onto the ball, at the same time raising the coupling-plunger.

3

When the coupling is attached securely to the ball, release the plunger. Then raise the jockey wheel to its maximum height.

I

Manoeuvre the car until its towing-ball is as near as possible to the caravan coupling. Release the caravan handbrake and guide the coupling over the ball.

4

Link up the safety cable or chain (if there is one) and finally plug in the electric cable.

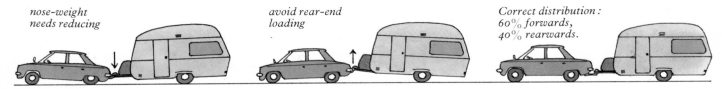

nose-weight needs reducing

avoid rear-end loading

Correct distribution: 60% forwards, 40% rearwards.

Otherwise the van may ride in an unstable manner during towing and even snake disconcertingly from side to side.

Generally, the recommended weight is around 10% of the caravan's all-up weight and it can be checked either with a special noseweight balance or by placing the jockeywheel on your bathroom scales. The weight also happens to be very close to that of an average-sized woman, so if the distribution of items on board is correct a couple may be able to devise their own day-to-day checking system: the wife only needs to place her weight on the back end while the husband sees how much the tow bar rises.

Once on the site, of course, you will be lowering the four adjustable legs that are set at the corners of the caravan in order to level it and act as stabilisers. These legs should never be used for jacking up the van, for instance when a wheel is removed.

Well before you set off on holiday it is also advisable to check your car's suspension. If you intend to carry a full load of passengers and to have a fully loaded boot in addition to what you stow in the caravan, you will usually find it sensible to fit a new pair of dampers (shock absorbers). At the same time you may also need to strengthen the springs by fitting spring assisters and then it will only be a matter of weight distribution to ensure that the car rides reasonably well and level.

Looking forward to reversing
A friendly hire company may allow you to hitch up to your chosen caravan for an hour or two before the actual day on which you start your holiday. If not, allow yourself plenty of time on the day of collection. You will need to complete the paperwork, check the inventory, see that the lights work when they are connected up and that a numberplate corresponding to your car's is attached. You should then practise for a while to get the feel of the van. Most good hirers will at least give you a short "crash" course to familiarise you with their vehicle.

Towing a caravan in a forward direction is not difficult. It just requires more time to accelerate through the gears and more attention to obstacles and

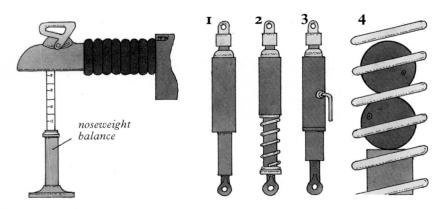

noseweight balance

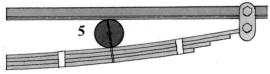

1 *Replacement shock absorber.*
2 *Shock absorber with strengthening spring.*
3 *Air-chamber shock absorber.*
4 *Inflated hollow spheres inserted in coil springs.*
5 *'Clamp-on' hollow sphere inserted between the suspension leaf-spring and the car body.*
   Another strengthening method is to add an extra leaf to the spring itself.

other road users. Cyclists and horseriders should be given a wide berth and if there are several vehicles behind you waiting to overtake, be prepared to pull in to the side of the road at a safe spot and let them go past. By doing this you may save someone from becoming impatient and taking an unnecessary risk. You are not likely to do too much overtaking of your own but remember that you need extra time and roadwidth for the operation and that except to avoid an accident you are not permitted to cross into the outside lane of a three-lane motorway.

The thought of having to reverse often sends shivers down the spine of first-time caravanners. In fact if you practise first in an unhurried situation it is quite fun to master the trick of doing so. In the first place, ask a companion to help with directing the rear

of the van and pushing back the release lever on the caravan's overrun brake mechanism. On many modern vans the overrun system is released automatically when the wheels turn backwards but on some models when you reverse you will naturally cause the brakes to clamp on unless they are specially held off. The release mechanism on the tow bar is designed to cancel itself as soon as you move forward again, so in a to and fro manoeuvre someone may have to pull back the lever by hand several times.

Apart from this slight complication with the braking system, there is really only one point to remember: that is to start each reverse turn by swinging the rear of the car a fraction in the opposite direction to the one in which you want to go. The accompanying illustrations show how this works.

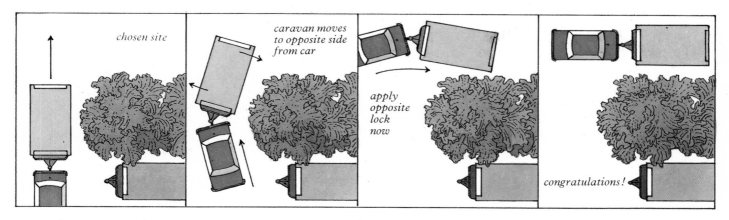

chosen site

caravan moves to opposite side from car

apply opposite lock now

congratulations!

The outdoor world is yours

Join a caravan club if you like; study the roadmaps they provide which pick out the narrow, difficult stretches you should avoid; certainly take along the club guide to caravan and camping sites in the area you intend to visit. But as you say goodbye to your everyday indoor life you are now on your own and at

the point where only experience itself can be a good teacher.

Whether you have invested in a caravan, piled your family and pets into a camper, packed a frame tent into the boot or lifted a rucksack onto your back, you have taken the decision to become independent for a while. That makes you something out of the ordinary and Heinz and Geneste Kurth wish you the best of freedom and success with your outdoor holiday. Send us a postcard, won't you?

index